Advanced Praise for *The Drucker Lectures*

"Peter Drucker shined a light in a dark and chaotic world, and his words remain as relevant today as when he first spoke them. Drucker's lectures and thoughts deserve to be considered by every person of responsibility, now, tomorrow, ten years from now, fifty, and a hundred."

—Jim Collins, author of *Good to Great*
and *How the Mighty Fall*

"Rick Wartzman has brought Peter Drucker alive again, and vividly so, in his own words. These samples of his talks and lectures, because they were spoken not written, will be new to almost all of us. A great and unexpected treat."

—Charles Handy, author of
Myself and Other More Important Matters

"Peter Drucker's ideas continue to resonate powerfully today. His lectures on effectiveness, innovation, the social sector, education and so much more provide fresh insights that extend beyond his other writings and provide lessons for us all. This book is a gem."

—Wendy Kopp, CEO and founder of Teach for America

"Rick Wartzman has performed a great service in pulling together *The Drucker Lectures*. The collection is as far-ranging as Drucker's thinking and writing. If you have sampled Drucker before, you will find things you haven't seen. Peter's ideas live on. You will be energized by reading them anew."

—Paul O'Neill, former U.S. Secretary of the Treasury

"Peter Drucker inspires awe. From the 1940s until his death a few years ago, he displayed a combination of insight, prescience, and productivity that few will ever match. This superbly edited collection captures both the range of Drucker's thinking and the sweep of history that informed it. *The Drucker Lectures* is a riveting read that reveals the depth and subtlety of one of America's most remarkable minds."

—Daniel H. Pink, author of
A Whole New Mind and *Drive*

"Rick Wartzman really has brought Peter to life in *The Drucker Lectures*. Reading this book, I practically felt as though I were seated in the audience, listening to my friend and hero, Peter Drucker—truly one of the great geniuses of management. These lectures are as vital today as they were when Peter delivered them. They cover significant territory, from the importance of faith and the individual to the rise of the global economy. It's a classic collection that belongs on every manager's bookshelf."

—Ken Blanchard, coauthor of
The One Minute Manager®
and *Leading at a Higher Level*

"Thank you, Rick Wartzman, for the pleasure of learning from the witty, informal Peter Drucker as his ideas unfold and his remarkable mind grapples with challenges of management that are still with us today."

—Rosabeth Moss Kanter,
Harvard Business School Professor
and author of *Confidence and SuperCorp:
How Vanguard Companies Create Innovation,
Profits, Growth, and Social Good*

The
DRUCKER
LECTURES

The

DRUCKER
LECTURES

ESSENTIAL LESSONS ON
MANAGEMENT, SOCIETY, AND ECONOMY

Peter F. Drucker

Edited and with an Introduction by
Rick Wartzman

New York   Chicago   San Francisco   Lisbon   London
Madrid   Mexico City   Milan   New Delhi   San Juan   Seoul
Singapore   Sydney   Toronto

1 2 3 4 5 6 7 8 9 10   WFR/WFR   1 5 4 3 2 1 0

ISBN 978-0-07-170045-0
MHID 0-07-170045-5

McGraw-Hill books are available at special quantity discounts to use as premiums and sales promotions or for use in corporate training programs. To contact a representative, please e-mail us at bulksales@mcgraw-hill.com.

CONTENTS

Part V
1980s

Part VI
1990s

Part VII
2000s 213

INTRODUCTION

You can picture him perched on the edge of a classroom table, peering through thick glasses at the students who hang on his every word. His baritone voice washes over the room, his Austrian accent as thick as a Sachertorte.

He doesn't refer to any written notes. But every now and again, his eyes roll back in his head and he pauses, almost like a computer downloading a store of information, before returning to his point and underscoring it with a new set of facts and figures.

His protean mind meanders from topic to topic—a discussion on cost accounting bleeding into a riff on Mesopotamian city-states before he veers into a lesson on the history of higher education or health care. But, somehow, he magically ties it all together in the end. In his hands, discursiveness becomes a fine art. And he delivers the entire talk with charm and humor and a genial style that, as one pupil has put it, recasts "the chilly lecture hall to the size and comfort of a living room."

Peter Drucker, widely hailed as the greatest management thinker of all time, is best known for the 39 books he wrote. Among them are such classics as *Concept of the Corporation* (1946); *The Practice of Management* (1954); *The Effective Executive* (1967); *Management: Tasks, Responsibilities, Practices* (1973); *Innovation and Entrepreneurship* (1985); and *Management Challenges for the 21st Century* (1999).

But those who had the pleasure of attending a Drucker lecture, before he died in 2005 just shy of his ninety-sixth birthday, got to see another side of him. Featuring lectures from the dawn of the television age straight through to the Internet age, from World War II to the aftermath of September 11, 2001, from the ascent into office of Chiang Kai-shek to the emergence of China as a global economic power, this book is designed to provide a taste of what that was like.

Drucker can be humble and self-deprecating in his comments, variously conceding: "I don't even know where to begin" and "I know I don't make sense." But mostly he is authoritative, speaking in absolutes. "Not one government program since 1950 has worked," he declares in a 1991 address at the Economic Club of Washington.

He can be shockingly bold. For example, in a 2001 lecture, Drucker goes so far as to call W. Edwards Deming, the quality guru, "totally obsolete." He can also push too far, suggesting in a 1997 speech on the changing world economy that "it is anybody's guess whether there will be a united Canada in 10 years."

Many of these lectures are notable for their erudition; an offhand reference to an eighteenth-century politician or a nineteenth-century novelist is not uncommon. At the same time, Drucker was never one to lose his head in the clouds. "Will you please be terribly nuts-and-bolts-focused in your questions," he requests at the end of a lecture at New York University in 1981, "because we have dealt in the stratosphere much too long."

Those acquainted with Drucker's oeuvre will find many familiar themes here: managing oneself, the value of volunteering, the need for every organization to focus on performance and results. At times, he'd use his lectures to test out ideas that would later find their way into print—the classroom serving as a kind of petri dish for his prose.

If there is a single subject that threads through this book it is one that Drucker spent the last half-century of his career contemplating: the historic shift from manufacturing to knowledge work. In these lectures, Drucker explores the implications of engaging our brains, instead of our brawn, from a variety of angles. He starts in 1957, where his remarks to an international management conference contain one of his earliest known references to "people who work by knowledge."

Yet there are also plenty of fresh insights—and more than a few surprises—to be found in these pages, even for the most diehard Drucker devotee. As a speaker, Drucker tends to be a bit less formal than in his writing. He is also apt to personalize his lectures, leavening his oratory with stories about his wife, Doris, his children, and his grandchildren. The shape of the audience can also make things interesting. It is one thing, for instance, for Drucker to hold forth on the vital importance of nonprofits. But this topic gets a new twist when he contextualizes his thinking for a group of Japanese.

Perhaps what makes this collection most remarkable, though, is the sheer span of time that it covers—a testament to Drucker's long and extraordinarily productive life. I have attempted to give a glimpse into the evolution of Drucker's philosophy by offering brief commentary at the beginning of each section of this book, which is divided by decade.

The first lecture here is from 1943, when Drucker was being billed in promotional materials as "stimulating and highly informative" but also as someone "with his feet on the ground," capable of communicating "in terms that the average businessman can understand and appreciate." The last lecture, when those exact same traits were still very much on display (even though Drucker's own hearing was then failing), came 60 years later, in 2003.

I selected these two talks, along with 31 others in between, with the help of Bridget Lawlor, the talented archivist at Claremont Graduate University's Drucker Institute. We looked, specifically, for lectures that hadn't been published before, at least not in book form. I then edited each one for clarity and readability. I have also tried to minimize the overlap among the lectures in this book; you should hear a few faint echoes, but no outright redundancies.

A handful of the lectures were given from behind a lectern, where Drucker left a polished text to draw from. But most were pulled from transcripts of videotapes of Drucker speaking more casually in the classroom, and with these I have taken considerably more liberties—cutting an immense amount of verbiage, moving pieces around, and composing new transitions. This was major surgery, not a minor cosmetic job, and these lectures are best thought of as "adapted from" rather than simply "excerpted from."

Purists may grumble about this approach. But anyone who wants to see the originals is welcome to visit Claremont to do so. In the meantime,

I have tried my best to make this collection accessible and enjoyable while abiding by a standard that Drucker believed should be the first responsibility of every manager but is sound advice for any editor, as well: Above all, do no harm.

Rick Wartzman
Claremont, Calif.

The

DRUCKER
LECTURES

Knowledge has to be improved, challenged, and increased constantly, or it vanishes.

—Peter F. Drucker

PART I

1940s

By the time the 1940s rolled around, many of the seminal events that would shape Peter Drucker's core philosophy had already unfolded. Most notably, the Nazis—who burned and banned some of Drucker's earliest writings—had swept across Europe, prompting the Austrian native to leave for England in 1933 and then immigrate to the United States in 1937. In between, while attending a Cambridge University lecture by economist John Maynard Keynes, he had an epiphany: "I suddenly realized that Keynes and all the brilliant economic students in the room were interested in the behavior of commodities while I was interested in the behavior of people." In 1939, Drucker wrote *The End of Economic Man*, exploring the rise of fascism on the continent he'd left behind. In 1942, he published *The Future of Industrial Man*. At its heart was the notion that the modern corporation had to justify its power and authority, while providing the individual with dignity, meaning, and status—bedrock beliefs that would infuse Drucker's writing for the next six decades. By dissecting the inner workings of a single enterprise, Drucker's work took on a new cast in 1946 with the release of *Concept of the Corporation*. The book examined General Motors not just as a business but also as a social entity that existed in the context of the broader community. Not everyone was impressed with this deep analysis of organization and management—topics that seemed to fall into a netherworld between politics and economics and that heretofore were largely unexplored. One reviewer expressed the hope that Drucker would "now devote his considerable talents to a more respectable subject." Thankfully, Drucker declined.

1

How Is Human Existence Possible?

1943

There has never been a century of Western history so far removed from an awareness of the tragic as that which bequeathed to us two world wars. It has trained all of us to suppress the tragic, to shut our eyes to it, to deny its existence.

Not quite 200 years ago—in 1755 to be exact—the death of 15,000 men in the Lisbon earthquake was enough to bring down the structure of traditional Christian belief in Europe. The contemporaries could not make sense of it. They could not reconcile this horror with the concept of an all-merciful God. And they could not see any answer to a catastrophe of such magnitude. Now, we daily learn of slaughter and destruction of vastly greater numbers, of whole peoples being starved or exterminated, of whole cities being leveled overnight. And it is far more difficult to explain these man-made catastrophes in terms of our nineteenth-century rationality than it was for the eighteenth century to explain the earthquake of Lisbon in the terms of the rationality of eighteenth-century Christianity. Yet I do not think that those contemporary catastrophes have shaken the optimism of these thousands of committees that are dedicated to the belief that permanent peace and prosperity will inevitably issue from this war. Sure, they are aware of the facts and are duly outraged by them. But they refuse to see them as catastrophes.

Yet however successful the nineteenth century was in suppressing the tragic in order to make possible human existence exclusively in time, there is one fact which could not be suppressed, one fact that remains outside of time: death. It is the one fact that cannot be made general but remains unique, the one fact that cannot be socialized but remains individual. The nineteenth century made every effort to strip death of its individual, unique, and qualitative aspect. It made death an incident in vital statistics, measurable quantitatively, predictable according to the natural laws of probability. It tried to get around death by organizing away its consequences. This is the meaning of life insurance, which promises to take the consequences out of death. Life insurance is perhaps the most representative institution of nineteenth-century metaphysics; for its promise "to spread the risks" shows most clearly the nature of this attempt to make death an incident in human life, instead of its termination.

It was the nineteenth century that invented Spiritualism with its attempt to control life after death by mechanical means. Yet death persists. Society might make death taboo, might lay down the rule that it is bad manners to speak of death, might substitute "hygienic" cremation for those horribly public funerals, and might call gravediggers "morticians." The learned Professor [Ernst] Haeckel [the German naturalist] might hint broadly that Darwinian biology is just about to make us live permanently; but he did not make good his promise. And as long as death persists, man remains with one pole of his existence outside of society and outside of time.

As long as death persists, the optimistic concept of life, the belief that eternity can be reached through time, and that the individual can fulfill himself in society can therefore have only one outcome: despair. There must come a point in the life of every man when he suddenly finds himself facing death. And at this point he is all alone; he is all individual. If he is lost, his existence becomes meaningless. [Danish philosopher and theologian Soren] Kierkegaard, who first diagnosed the phenomenon and predicted where it would lead to, called it the "despair at not willing to be an individual." Superficially the individual can recover from this encounter with the problem of existence in eternity. He may even forget it for a while. But he can never regain his confidence in his existence in society: Basically he remains in despair.

Society must thus attempt to make it possible for man to die if it wants him to be able to live exclusively in society. There is only one way in which society can do that: by making individual life itself meaningless. If you are nothing but a leaf on the tree, a cell in the body of society, then your death is not really a death; it is only a part of the life of the whole. You can hardly even talk of death; you better call it a process of collective regeneration. But then, of course, your life is not real life, either; it is just a functional process within the life of the whole, devoid of any meaning except in terms of the whole.

Thus you can see what Kierkegaard saw clearly a hundred years ago: that the optimism of a creed that proclaims human existence as existence in society must lead straight to despair, and that the despair leads straight to totalitarianism. And you can also see that the essence of the totalitarian creed is not how to live, but how to die. To make death bearable, individual life has to be made worthless and meaningless. The optimistic creed that starts out by making life in this world mean everything leads straight to the Nazi glorification of self-immolation as the only act in which man can meaningfully exist. Despair becomes the essence of life itself.

The nineteenth century thus reached the very point the pagan world had reached in the age of Euripides or in that of the late Roman Empire. And like antiquity, it tried to find a way out by escaping into the purely ethical, by escaping into virtue as the essence of human existence. Ethical Culture and that brand of liberal Protestantism that sees in Jesus the "best man ever lived," the Golden Rule and Kant's "Categorical Imperative," the satisfaction of service—those and other formulations of an ethical concept of life became as familiar in the nineteenth century as most of them had been in antiquity. And they failed to provide a basis for human existence as much as they had failed 2,000 years ago. In its noblest adherents the ethical concept leads to a stoic resignation, which gives courage and steadfastness but does not give meaning either to life or to death. And its futility is shown by its reliance upon suicide as the ultimate remedy—though to the stoic, death is the end of everything and of all existence. Kierkegaard rightly considered this position to be one of even greater despair than the optimistic one; he calls it "the despair at willing to be an individual."

In most cases, however, the ethical position does not lead to anything as noble and as consistent as the Stoic philosophy. Normally it is nothing but sugarcoating on the pill of totalitarianism. Or the ethical position becomes pure sentimentalism—the position of those who believe that evil can be abolished, harmony be established by the spreading of sweetness, light, and goodwill.

And in all cases the ethical position is bound to degenerate into our pure relativism. For if virtue is to be found in man, everything that is accepted by man must be virtue. Thus a position that starts out—as did Rousseau and Kant 175 years ago—to establish man-made ethical absolutes must end in John Dewey and in the complete denial of the possibility of an ethical position. This way, there is no escape from despair.

Is it then our conclusion that human existence cannot be an existence in tragedy and despair? If so, then the sages of the East are right who see in the destruction of the self, in the submersion of man into the Nirvana, the nothingness, the only answer.

Nothing could be further from Kierkegaard. For Kierkegaard has an answer. Human existence is possible as existence not in despair, as existence not in tragedy—it is possible as existence in faith. The opposite of Sin—to use the traditional term for existence purely in society—is not virtue; it is faith.

Faith is the belief that in God the impossible is possible, that in Him time and eternity are one, that both life and death are meaningful. In my favorite among Kierkegaard's books, a little volume called *Fear and Trembling* [published in 1843], Kierkegaard raises the question: What is it that distinguishes Abraham's willingness to sacrifice his son, Isaac, from ordinary murder?

If the distinction would be that Abraham never intended to go through with the sacrifice but intended all the time only to make a show of his obedience to God, then Abraham indeed would not have been a murderer, but he would have been something more despicable: a fraud and a cheat. If he had not loved Isaac but had been indifferent, he would have been willing to be a murderer. But Abraham was a holy man, and God's command was for him an absolute command to be executed without reservation. And we are told that he loved Isaac more than himself. But Abraham had faith. He believed that in God the impossible would become possible, that he could execute God's order and yet retain Isaac.

If you looked into this little volume on *Fear and Trembling*, you may have seen from the introduction of the translator that it deals symbolically with Kierkegaard's innermost secret, his great and tragic love. When he talks of himself, then he talks of Abraham. But this meaning as a symbolic autobiography is only incidental. The true, the universal meaning is that human existence is possible, only possible, in faith. In faith, the individual becomes the universal, ceases to be isolated, becomes meaningful and absolute; hence in faith there is a true ethic. And in faith existence in society becomes meaningful too as existence in true charity.

This faith is not what today so often is called a "mystical experience"—something that can apparently be induced by the proper breathing exercises, by fasting, by narcotic drugs or by prolonged exposure to Bach with closed eyes and closed ears. It is something that can be attained only through despair, through tragedy, through long, painful, and ceaseless struggle. It is not irrational, sentimental, emotional, or spontaneous. It comes as the result of serious thinking and learning, of rigid discipline, of complete sobriety, absolute will. It is something few can attain; but all can—and should—search for it.

This is as far as I can go. If you want to go further, if you want to know about the nature of religious experience, about the way to it, about faith itself, you have to read Kierkegaard. Even so, you may say that I have tried to lead you further than I know the road myself. You may reproach me for trying to make Kierkegaard accept society as real and meaningful whereas he actually repudiated it. You may even say that I have failed in relating faith to existence in society. All these complaints would be justified, but I would not be very much disturbed by them—at least not as far as the purpose of this talk is concerned. For all I wanted to show you is the possibility that we have a philosophy that enables men to die. Do not underestimate the strength of such a philosophy. For in a time of great sorrow and catastrophe such as we have to live through, it is a great thing to be able to die. But it is not enough. Kierkegaard too enables men to die; but his faith also enables them to live.

From a lecture delivered at Bennington College, where Drucker had joined the faculty in 1942.

2

The Myth of the State

1947

The word *myth* is a very queer word. If you look it up in the dictionary, you will find it defined as "a tale, a fabrication, usually invoking the supernatural to explain natural phenomena." This definition is literally correct, or at least as correct as a dictionary definition can hope to be. You can test it for yourself; just see how neatly it fits the "myth of the state" we're going to talk about tonight.

And yet the rhetorical emphasis on the definition and its propagandistic aim are the exact opposite of what we today usually mean when we talk about the myth. What the standard definition conveys is that myth is a silly superstition, an old wives' tale. At best, it is tolerated as a harmless flight of fancy, as an ornament, a glittering trinket for children or for the leisure hours of the tired businessman. At worst, it is condemned as the invention of unscrupulous quacks—greedy priests, power-hungry demagogues, ruthless capitalists—who use it to frighten the gullible, uneducated, and stupid into submission and tribute.

Now, I am not saying that myth cannot be abused or misused—in fact, in talking about the myth of the state the main questions are precisely: What is the proper, the right use of the myth? And what is demagogic, obscurantist, tyrannical misuse? But when we use the term *myth*, we are nevertheless not talking about a superstition or an old wives' tale. We talk about something that is real, rational, and true: the symbolical expression of an experience common to all men.

The radical change in the connotation of the term means a radical change in basic philosophical concepts and beliefs and, above all, in the concept of human nature. It's a shift from a philosophy that sees man as reason, with the rest of his being—body, emotion, experience—either as an illusion or a weakness, to a philosophical position which again attempts to see all of man, that is, to see a being.

The myth, as even the extreme eighteenth-century rationalists saw, deals with experience. It deals with what we know, not with what we can deduce or prove. Experience is not reason; it is experience. To the Cartesian rationalist and to his successor, the German idealist philosopher, reality, truth, and validity existed only in reason, and reason could only be applied to what was in reason to begin with. There was no bridge from the truth of reason to the illusions and phantasma of experience. Experience was not just nonrational; it was irrational. And the myth was worse: It was a lie.

Every myth attempts to present the nonrational experience in a form in which reason can go to work on it. And that, to the rationalist or idealist, is, from his point of view, the worst crime; it is a dishonesty, which can only have the purpose of enslaving reason.

The moment, however, we see man again as a being—as a creature that has existence rather than as an isolated particle of reason—the myth becomes central. The myth symbolizing it opens experience to reason. It makes it possible for reason to understand and to analyze our experience, to criticize, direct, and change our reaction to experience. Instead of being irrational, the myth is seen as a great rationalizer—the bridge between experience and reason.

The myth makes it possible for our reason to order experience in a rational, meaningful way—that is, it makes possible the ritual. It enables our reason to direct and to determine our reaction to experience. By making us understand what it is we know from our experience, it makes possible action, which is our term for movement directed by reason, when otherwise there would only have been superstition. Without the myth, we would be slaves to panic; the myth enables man to walk upright; it liberates his reason from the nameless terror of the incomprehensible outside and in.

It is because it is so real, so central, so potent, that I say, "Beware of the Myth." Because it is the basis of all ritual and of all institutions, it is all-important that it be a true myth, truly interpreted. For a false myth, or one that is interpreted falsely, is the most vicious, the most destructive thing we know. But you may ask, how can a myth be true or false? Isn't it an open contradiction to apply such philosophical or ethical value terms to experience? But the myth is not just experience; it is the symbolical expression of experience, which means that the myth itself is already a product of our consciousness, of our reason, of our beliefs, the product of a decision as to what is relevant in our experience and what our experience actually means. And this applies with even greater force to the interpretation of the myth—that is, to ritual and action.

You can say that any myth is a valid myth if it has stood the pragmatic test, the test of time. It could not have survived unless it expressed in a plausible symbol an experience common to the human species. The myth always raises the right questions, always registers the right seismic disturbances, but it does not by necessity give the right answers. In fact, it gives no answers at all. The answers are given by our interpretation of the myth and of the experience it expresses; they are given, in brief, by philosophy and theology, the two disciplines that are exclusively concerned with the analysis, interpretation, and critique of the basic myth. These answers may be right, but they may also be wrong, depending upon the principles, methods, and aims of the philosopher and theologian.

All this, as you may now have realized, has been by way of introduction to my assignment tonight, to speak on the "Myth of the State." The people who first talked of the state as a myth did not understand the term to mean what I make it mean. On the contrary, by calling the state a myth they meant to say that there really is no such thing as a state, that there are only individuals existing by themselves, and that it is a lie and worse to pretend that there is a state. Nevertheless, the state is a true myth in the sense in which I have been using the term.

The experience of belonging to a group, the experience that the group is real, has existence and has definite qualities and, you might even say, has a body, is one every one of us has had. And we also know, beyond rational proof and beyond contradiction, that there are situations in which this phenomenon we call "group" has more reality and more life than the individual, situations in which the individual is willing to die so that the group may live. You may try to explain this phenomenon rationally and develop the state from the biological necessity of the family to care for infant and nursing mother, or from the utilitarian principle that half a loaf is better than no bread at all. But you won't get very far this way. Certainly you could not explain rationally that central political experience, the experience we call "allegiance." You can only deny that there is such a basic experience, that there is anything but the individual—but that makes little more sense than to deny any other basic experience, such as that of our senses; it also makes you incapable of any political effectiveness and action. If you are in politics, you must accept the reality of the organized group as a basic experience of man's life. You must accept the myth of the state as a real myth, as a symbolical expression of a genuine experience, common to all of us.

And it is a real myth, according even to the dictionary definition I gave you at the beginning: "a tale, a fabrication, invoking the supernatural to explain a natural phenomenon." We may not consciously personify the state as supernatural, though the process that gave us the person of Uncle Sam and the symbolism of the flag is probably not so very different from that that gave our ancestors the corn goddess or the sacred oak of Dodona. But even without the externals of personification, we see the state as a supernatural being. We endow it with immortality and, though we cannot see it, we give it reality and effectiveness, which means that we give it the invisible body of the supernatural. All this, however, does not mean, as the rationalists thought, that we deal with a mere superstition, which dissolves before the light of logic and reason. It means, on the contrary, that we are up against a reality and that the myth alone makes it possible for us to deal with it rationally.

It makes no sense, then, to question whether there is a state or whether there should be one. The very fact that we have the myth of the state shows that the only question that is meaningful is: What myth should we have, and how should we interpret it, to have a true myth and a true state?

Often the answers have been given in an indirect form—that is, by changing the title of the myth, by putting a different term for *state*: tribe, polis, society, law, nation, race, etc. Of course, each new title starts out with a different meaning and is brought in with a definite propagandistic purpose. But very soon the same old questions come up in connection with the new title, which, to answer once and for all, the new title had been devised for. Hence we have always been forced to do the job the hard way: by working out the answers ourselves.

This job of working out the answers has been the central, perhaps the only problem of political philosophy over the ages. Therefore, I can hardly be expected to give you the solution in the few minutes left to me tonight.

But there seem to me to be implicit in the fact that it is a myth certain absolute prerequisites for a true interpretation of the myth of the state. First, the organized group is undoubtedly a reality, not a fiction, an elementary experience, not something deduced, derived, or secondary. Man is by nature a social animal, a "zoon politikon" [Aristotle's term for a social or political creature]. He does not exist except in the group. Any interpretation of the myth that does not accept this seems to me *prima facie* invalid and untrue, and likely to lead to untold harm.

But secondly, the very fact that we have a myth of the state—that is, that we can rationalize our experience—also shows that man is not all political animal, and that his existence is not described or circumscribed by his belonging to the group. Ants and bees are as much social animals as man. An ant or a bee can even overthrow the ruler of the swarm and establish his own rulership. But only man can change the basic order of the group itself, only man has the myth of the state. Hence man is also and always not a political animal that exists in the group; he also and always exists outside the group as an individual.

Finally, the myth of the state expresses always the nonbelonging, the nonallegiance to all the other groups. It establishes a group ritual, it leads to group action, but at the same time it excludes from group ritual and opposes group action. Yet the very fact that it is universal myth expressing an experience common to all men—black, brown, and white, American, Russian, or Hottentot—shows conclusively that, as in all other essential experiences of human existence, we are alike in our political experience.

No myth of the state, I submit, could be a true myth or be truly interpreted unless it expressed the fact of separation of group from group. But no myth of the state could be a true one unless it also expressed our common humanity. In fine, the myth of the state, to be a true myth, truly interpreted, has to express symbolically the polarity of human existence. And, in the last analysis, to express symbolically that man is a dual being by his nature—animal and individual at the same time—is the basic purpose of all myth.

From a lecture delivered at Bennington College.

PART II

1950s

Business historian Alfred D. Chandler Jr. has described the 1950s as a "Golden Age of Capitalism" in which big American companies fueled economic growth by exploiting "new knowledge-intensive as well as capital-intensive technologies in chemistry, pharmaceuticals, aircraft, and electronics." One can easily add to that list another innovation of the era: management. And more than anyone, it was Peter Drucker who showed the way. His 1954 book, *The Practice of Management*, became the guide to which countless executives turned in order to master the basics: "What is our business and what should it be?" "Management by objectives and self-control." "The spirit of an organization." "Motivating to peak performance." Years later, management scholar Jim Collins would note that when he dug into the backgrounds of "visionary companies" such as General Electric, Johnson & Johnson, Procter & Gamble, Hewlett-Packard, Merck, and Motorola, he discovered Drucker's "intellectual fingerprints" everywhere. "David Packard's notes and speeches from the foundation years at HP so mirrored Drucker's writings," Collins said, "that I conjured an image of Packard giving management sermons with a classic Drucker text in hand." Drucker himself said that, after 10 years of consulting and teaching, he was simply filling a void with *The Practice of Management*. Nothing like it existed. "So I kind of sat down and wrote it, very conscious of the fact that I was laying the foundations of a discipline." By the end of the decade, Drucker had also coined a new term: "knowledge worker." And he would spend the rest of his days contemplating the ways in which knowledge had supplanted land, labor, and capital as "the one critical factor of production."

3

The Problems of Maintaining Continuous and Full Employment

1957

There are three major forces in an industrial economy today that exert pressure toward making employment continuous and stable:

- The first is social pressure, especially through organized trade unions. Some suggest that it is natural that the worker should give stable employment first place among his cares and hopes. In the United States, this is a considerable overstatement; such things as wage levels, working hours, and opportunities for advancement are likely to rank as high among the "care and hopes" of many workers in this country as does stable employment. And while "natural," stable employment is a recent concern of the worker. Only 30 years ago, wages and working conditions would have undoubtedly been given "first place," and stability of employment might, a generation ago, not have been among the conscious cares of the worker at all. We face, in other words, a basic change in the goals and aspirations of the worker in industrial society—and perhaps a change that offers opportunities as well as challenges of management.
- The next major pressure toward maintaining continuous and stable employment is modern production technology, both

in manufacturing and in distribution. The trend toward the highly capitalized plant or store sharply limits the adaptability of productive facilities to short-term fluctuations in demand. Specifically, a larger and larger part of the workforce—whether rank and file or managerial, technical, or professional—has to be kept on regardless of the volume of production, as long as the facility itself is being operated at all. Labor costs, in other words, are rapidly moving from the category of "variable" to that of "fixed."

• Finally—and in the long run perhaps the most important element in this situation—business increasingly employs people who are highly trained and who do technical, professional, and managerial work. Rapidly the workforce is shifting from being composed primarily of manual workers, whether skilled or unskilled, to being largely composed of people who work by knowledge. This workforce represents increasingly years of training and development within the enterprise itself. It increasingly brings to bear on its work what is often literally irreplaceable knowledge, experience, and skills. The investment in the training and development of these men—though hidden by our traditional accounting concepts—is often higher than the capital in machines and tools invested per man. The enterprise cannot easily accept the dispersion of this, its major capital resource. On the contrary, it must increasingly try to maintain this capital resource together and in its own employment. For once laid off, these people may never come back.

In conclusion, it might be said that where today the drive for continuous and stable employment seems primarily to be propelled by social pressures and carried by organized labor unions, tomorrow—and this tomorrow in a highly developed country like the United States may only be 10 years off—the pressure for continuous and stable employment will increasingly come from within the business enterprise itself and will express its own technological, economic, and manpower needs.

The problems that these pressures raise can be summarized under four headings:

- How, if employment is maintained, can the solvency of the individual enterprise and its financial integrity be preserved and safeguarded through cyclical fluctuations?
- What impact on productivity is a stable-employment or stable-income policy likely to have?
- How can employment be stabilized in such a manner as to avoid harmful effects on the stability of the economy, on its development, and on its growth? In particular, how can employment be stabilized without creating inflationary forces? What will this effect be on adaptability of the economy and of the employee to technological change, and how can we avoid abuse of any employment stabilization to prevent technological progress and technological change?
- What is the impact on the mobility of the economy and of the individual within it? How will it affect individual opportunities and individual freedom of movement? How will it affect the individual's ability to find a new job if enterprises are committed to maintaining the employment of present employees? What about the danger that the individual, because of "security of employment," will stay on even where he is not best placed, either in respect to his opportunities, in respect to the contribution he can make, or in respect to his ability, knowledge, and skill?

So far in the United States only the first of these problems has even been considered—and even that only quite superficially. It is my personal opinion that this represents a definite shortcoming in our vision and approach and that, within the next 10 to

20 years, the other three problem areas are likely to become a good deal more important. They threaten to present greater difficulties and greater dangers than the danger to the solvency of the enterprise and its financial integrity, important though this undoubtedly is.

By and large there have been three major approaches to the task of providing stable and continuous employment in the United States. All three focus on the rank-and-file employee and especially on the unionized employee.

The first of these approaches attempts to provide greater stability in the operations of a company. This can be attempted in several ways, which very often can be tackled concurrently. One of these—the easiest and most productive wherever it applies— is to smooth out those internal operations that are largely not affected by fluctuations in business and consumer demand. One example would be the maintenance expenditures of a railroad, which are primarily dictated by the need to maintain intact and in good working order the railroad's business—producing assets. In fact, it has been shown that railroad maintenance work is done most efficiently and most cheaply in times of slack business. It can be said that any success in smoothing out such internal operation is beneficial all around, in addition to being usually quite profitable for the enterprise itself.

Another approach is to try to smooth out fluctuations in employment by using internal operations—such as maintenance— as a counterweight to operations for market and consumer. This was, incidentally, the line taken by the earlier attempts to provide "guaranteed employment" in this country. In the meatpacking firm of Hormel, for instance, maintenance work is deferred until there are slack times in factory employment, and factory workers are then used to do maintenance work.

The next line of attack would be one that directly tackles such predictable short-term fluctuations and tries to maintain production regardless of such fluctuations and in anticipation of a stable "cycle." This is probably, from the point of view of the individual enterprise, a more promising line of attack than the shift of production workers to maintenance workers to maintenance work and back again.

Another line of attack, under the same heading of smoothing out internal operations, is to smooth out fluctuations in the economy caused by unnecessarily fluctuating demand of the company itself. While this does nothing to smooth out fluctuations in demand in the enterprise itself, it contributes to the stability of employment throughout the economy. In fact, there is little doubt that the remarkable stability of employment in the American economy during the last few years is, to a large extent, the result of the adoption of long-range planning for capital expenditures on the part of more and more businesses.

Finally, a company can attempt to create conditions of stability in its own market by planning and developing the market, by anticipating and predicting it, and by creating organized systematic innovation and a pricing policy that will encourage continuous demand on the part of its own customers. This presupposes an expanding economy. It involves entrepreneurial risk taking. It must be based on the application of systematic and scientific methods of management. And finally, it presupposes creative, imaginative, and aggressive marketing.

There is the danger with this last approach that results will be sought through methods that restrict the market and create monopolistic and artificial limitations in it. It must, therefore, be stressed that under conditions of modern technology such an attempt to get the benefits of market stability without the risks of competitive and aggressive market creation simply will not work.

The second basic approach to this task of providing stable and continuous employment in the United States is through guaranteeing to individuals a preference—right in their jobs. In a great many cases, this amounts to virtually complete job security. The means to do this is, of course, "seniority" according to which, in any layoff or dismissal, workers will be laid off or dismissed in the reverse of their length of service with the company (or, in some cases, with the industry).

Seniority provisions in American industry exist in a great variety of forms and detail as they are being set by individual union agreements. They actually exist also outside of unionized industry—by custom rather than by contract, but nevertheless in highly binding form. As mentioned, they mean that employees with two to five years of service, according to company or industry (and in practically all cases this would embrace about two-thirds of all employees), enjoy virtual job security as long as the company keeps in operation.

The disadvantages of any seniority system are very well known and need no repetition here. It is, however, only rarely understood that seniority is a principle of guaranteeing employment—and an exceedingly effective one.

Our final approach, developed only within the last few years, is to guarantee not a job and employment but the maintenance of income. This is the aim of the various plans known as "supplementary unemployment benefit plans," which have become so prominent in American industry during the last few years—even though the first one, between the United Auto Workers union and the leading automobile companies, was concluded only two years ago in the spring of 1955.

With the exception of the seniority approach—which has been with Western industry for at least a hundred years—U.S. experience differs considerably from approaches to the same problem in many other countries. The biggest difference is obviously that in the United States the problem is considered primarily one of private industry to be solved through individual negotiations with individual labor unions. In other countries—

in Italy, for instance, but also in Great Britain—it is to be solved by social legislation or government supervision.

Another basic characteristic of the American approach is, increasingly, at least for rank-and-file employees, stabilization of income rather than guarantee of employment is in the center of our effort. Finally—albeit, with significant exceptions, especially in such industries as the railroads—there has been very little or no attempt to slow down or to limit technological or managerial advance and change in order to preserve jobs.

To a very large extent these are characteristics that typify American economic conditions and industrial relations. But they might very well express specific experiences of great importance not only to this country but to all countries.

First, they are likely to express our experience—which organized labor in this country has by and large learned, too—that technological progress and greater productivity do not endanger jobs but create jobs. This is not to say that there is no such thing as "technological unemployment." But it is a marginal rather than a central problem. And our experience has been that by and large increased productivity means a larger rather than a smaller labor force.

It means, however, very often jobs requiring greater skill or knowledge—that is, an upgrading of the labor force. This is particularly true of the shift to automation. One of our experiences is, therefore, that maintaining jobs and even maintaining income are no substitute for managerial effort to retrain employees for new responsibilities arising out of technological advance; in fact, any attempt to use guarantees of employment or income as a substitute for such a constructive approach toward making the worker ready for new and usually better-paid and more responsible jobs would be a serious and dangerous misuse.

The second specific experience that underlies the American approach is probably that the easiest way to make "technological unemployment" a real danger is to try to prevent technological change. This only makes certain that technological change, when it comes, will be catastrophic change.

And, finally, the American approach raises the question whether there is not a great deal more actual "job security" in the American system—and, by inference, in any economy that consciously and systematically works on its own constant expansion—than is customarily recognized.

Studies have shown that even during the Great Depression—and even during 1937–1938, when we had the most rapid decline in productions and employment—70 percent or more of the workers of the great majority of enterprises were in no danger of losing their jobs and usually not even in danger of having to work short time, except for a week or two at a stretch. Another way of saying this is that even during the Depression, management in the United States had a serious problem of "turnover"—that is, of voluntary quits despite the great and understandable fear for job security that pervaded the employees.

In other words, the problem is perhaps not so much that of changing the pattern of industry from one of great built-in employment instability to one of greater stability. The problem might very well be that of bringing out, making visible, and institutionalizing an already existing very high degree of job stability in such a manner that it strengthens the individual enterprise, strengthens the economy, advances productivity, and advances the individual's opportunities and freedom.

From remarks submitted to the Eleventh International Management Congress in Paris, on behalf of the American delegation.

PART III

1960s

Jack Beatty, Peter Drucker's biographer, has pointed out that, in spite of its provocative title, Drucker's 1968 book *The Age of Discontinuity* "all but ignores" the most convulsive events of the day: student protests, the Civil Rights movement, and Vietnam. And yet, he added, *The Age of Discontinuity* is "a very 1960s book in its conviction that truth lies under the surface" and "trends under the trends." Specifically, what Drucker set out to chronicle were big, if little noticed, changes in the "social and cultural reality" that seemed likely "to mold and shape the closing decades of the twentieth century." Among the "new industries already in sight," Drucker proclaimed, was one called "information systems." "The impact of cheap, reliable, fast, and universally available information," he wrote, "will easily be as great as was the impact of electricity. Certainly young people, a few years hence, will use information systems as their normal tools, much as they now use the typewriter or the telephone." Of course, few people besides Drucker could see all this back then. But Drucker wasn't only profound and prescient. He was also practical—a trait exhibited in another Drucker classic of the decade, *The Effective Executive*, published in 1967. By teaching principles of time management, the elements of decision making, and building on one's strengths, Drucker showcased his ability to share insights on an altogether different level: not that of society or the organization, but of the individual practitioner striving to "manage oneself."

4

The First Technological Revolution
and Its Lessons

1965

Aware that we are living in the midst of a technological revolution, we are becoming increasingly concerned with its meaning for the individual and its impact on freedom, on society, and on our political institutions. Side by side with messianic promises of utopia to be ushered in by technology, there are the most dire warnings of man's enslavement by technology, his alienation from himself and from society, and the destruction of all human and political values.

Tremendous though today's technological explosion is, it is hardly greater than the first great revolution technology wrought in human life 7,000 years ago when the first great civilization of man, the irrigation civilization, established itself. First in Mesopotamia, and then in Egypt and in the Indus Valley, and finally in China, there appeared a new society and a new polity: the irrigation city, which then rapidly became the irrigation empire. No other change in man's way of life and in his making a living, not even the changes underway today, so completely revolutionized human society and community. In fact, the irrigation civilizations were the beginning of history, if only because they brought writing. The age of the irrigation civilization was preeminently an age of technological innovation. Not until a historical yesterday, the eighteenth century, did technological innovations emerge which were comparable in their scope and impact to those early changes in technology, tools, and processes. Indeed, the technology of man remained essentially unchanged until the eighteenth century insofar as its impact on human life and human society is concerned.

But the irrigation civilizations were not only one of the great ages of technology. They represent also mankind's greatest and most productive age of social and political innovation. The historian of ideas is prone to go back to Ancient Greece, to the Old Testament prophets, or to the China of the early dynasties for the sources of the beliefs that still move men to action. But our fundamental social and political institutions antedate political philosophy by several thousand years. They all were conceived and established in the early dawn of the irrigation civilizations. Anyone interested in social and governmental institutions and in social and political processes will increasingly have to go back to those early irrigation cities. And, thanks to the work of archaeologists and linguists during the last 50 years, we increasingly have the information, we increasingly know what the irrigation civilizations looked like, we increasingly can go back to them for our understanding both of antiquity and of modern society.

The irrigation city first established government as a distinct and permanent institution. Even more basic: The irrigation city first conceived of man as a citizen. It had to go beyond the narrow bounds of tribe and clan and had to weld people of very different origins and blood into one community. The irrigation city also first developed a standing army. It had to, for the farmer was defenseless and vulnerable and, above all, immobile.

It was in the irrigation city that social classes first developed. It needed people permanently engaged in producing the farm products on which all the city lived; it needed farmers. It needed soldiers to defend them. And it needed a governing class with knowledge—originally a priestly class. Down to the end of the nineteenth century, these three "estates" were still considered basic in society. But at the same time, the irrigation city went in for specialization of labor, resulting in the emergence of artisans and craftsmen (potters, weavers, metalworkers, and so on) and of professional people (scribes, lawyers, judges, physicians).

And because it produced a surplus, it first engaged in organized trade, which brought with it not only the merchant but money, credit, and a law that extended beyond the city to give protection, predictability, and justice to the stranger, the trader from far away.

The irrigation city first had knowledge, organized it, and institutionalized it. Both because it required considerable knowledge to construct and maintain the complex engineering works that regulated the vital water supply and because it had to manage complex economic transactions stretching over many years and over hundreds of miles, the irrigation city needed records, and this, of course, meant writing. It needed astronomical data, as it depended on a calendar. It needed means of navigating across sea or desert. It, therefore, had to organize both the supply of the needed information and its processing into learnable and teachable knowledge. As a result, the irrigation city developed the first schools and the first teachers.

Finally, the irrigation city created the individual. Outside the city, as we can still see from those tribal communities that have survived to our days, only the tribe had existence. The individual as such was neither seen nor paid attention to. In the irrigation city of antiquity, however, the individual became, of necessity, the focal point. And with this emerged not only compassion and the concept of justice; with it emerged the arts as we know them, the poets, and eventually the religions and the philosophers.

This is, of course, not even the barest sketch. All I wanted to stress is that the irrigation city was essentially "modern," as we have understood the term, and that until today history largely consisted of building on the foundations laid 5,000 or more years ago. In fact, one can argue that human history, in the last 5,000 years, has largely been an extension of the social and political institutions of the irrigation city to larger and larger areas—that is, to all areas of the globe where water supply is adequate for the systematic tilling of the soil.

The irrigation civilization was based squarely upon a technological revolution. It can, with justice, be called a "technological polity." All its institutions were responses to opportunities and challenges that new technology offered. All its institutions were essentially aimed at making the new technology most productive.

So, what can we learn from the first technological revolution regarding the impacts likely to result on man, his society, and his government from the new industrial revolution, the one we are living in? Does the story of the irrigation civilization show man to be determined by his technical achievements, in thrall to them, coerced by them? Or does it show him capable of using technology to human ends and of being the master of the tools of his own devising?

Without a shadow of doubt, major technological change creates the need for social and political innovation. It does make obsolete existing institutional arrangements. It does require new and very different institutions of community, society, and government. To this extent there can be no doubt: Technological change of a revolutionary character coerces; it demands innovation—specific social and political innovation.

In other words, one lesson to be learned from the first technological revolution is that new technology creates what a philosopher of history might call "objective reality." And objective reality has to be dealt with on *its* terms. Such a reality would, for instance, be the conversion, in the course of the first technological revolution, of human space from "habitat" into "settlement"—

that is, into a permanent territorial unit always to be found in the same place, unlike the migrating herds of pastoral people or the hunting grounds of primitive tribes. This alone made obsolete the tribe and demanded a permanent, impersonal, and rather powerful government.

But the irrigation civilizations can teach us also that the new objective reality determines only the gross parameters of the solutions. It determines where, and in respect to what, new institutions are needed. It does not make anything "inevitable." It leaves wide open how the new problems are being tackled, what the purpose and values of the new institutions are to be. Even within the Old World, where one irrigation civilization could learn from the others, there were very great differences. They were far from homogeneous, even though all had similar tasks to accomplish and developed similar institutions for these tasks.

Impersonal bureaucratic government had to arise in all these civilizations; without it they could not have functioned. But in the Near East it was seen at a very early stage that such a government could serve equally to exploit and hold down the common man and to establish justice for all and protection for the weak. From the beginning, the Near East saw an ethical decision as crucial to government. In Egypt, however, this decision was never seen. The question of the purpose of government was never asked. And the central quest of government in China was not justice but harmony.

It was in Egypt that the individual first emerged, as witness the many statues, portraits, and writings of professional men, such as scribes and administrators, that have come down to us— most of them superbly aware of the uniqueness of the individual and clearly asserting his primacy. But Egypt suppressed the individual after a fairly short period during which he flowered (perhaps as part of the reaction against the dangerous heresies of Ikhnaton [a pharaoh who had abandoned traditional polytheistic religious practices]). There is no individual left in the records of the Middle and New Kingdoms, which perhaps explains their relative sterility.

In the other areas two entirely different basic approaches emerged. One, that of Mesopotamia and of the Taoists, we might call "personalism," the approach that found its greatest expression later in the Hebrew prophets and in the Greek dramatists. Here the stress is on developing to the fullest the capacities of the person. In the other approach—we might call it "rationalism," taught and exemplified above all by Confucius—the aim is the molding and shaping of the individual according to pre-established ideals of rightness and perfection. I need not tell you that both these approaches still permeate our thinking about education.

Or take the military. Organized defense was a necessity for the irrigation civilization. But three different approaches emerged: a separate military class supported through tribute by the producing class, the farmers; the citizen-army drafted from the peasantry itself; and mercenaries.

Even the class structure, though it characterizes all irrigation civilizations, showed great differences from culture to culture and within the same culture at different times. It was being used to create permanent castes and complete social immobility, but it was also used with great skill to create a very high degree of social mobility and a substantial measure of opportunities for the gifted and ambitious.

For the first time in thousands of years, we face again a situation that can be compared with what our remote ancestors faced at the time of the irrigation civilization. It is not only the speed of technological change that creates a revolution; it is its scope as well. Above all, today, as 7,000 years ago, technological developments from a great many areas are growing together to create a new human environment. This has not been true of any period between the first technological revolution and the technological revolution that got underway 200 years ago and has still clearly not run its course.

We, therefore, face a big task of identifying the areas in which social and political innovations are needed. We face a big task in developing the institutions for the new tasks, institutions adequate to the new needs and to the new capacities which technological change is casting up. And, finally, we face the biggest task of them all—the task of ensuring that the new institutions embody the values we believe in, aspire to the purposes we consider right, and serve human freedom, human dignity, and human ends.

If an educated man of those days of the first technological revolution—an educated Sumerian, perhaps, or an educated ancient Chinese—looked at us today, he would certainly be totally stumped by our technology. But he would, I am sure, find our existing social and political institutions reasonably familiar. They are, after all, by and large not fundamentally different from the institutions he and his contemporaries first fashioned.

And, I am quite certain, he would have nothing but a wry smile for both those among us who predict a technological heaven and those who predict a technological hell of "alienation," of "technological unemployment," and so on. He might well mutter to himself, "This is where I came in." But to us he might well say, "A time such as was mine and such as is yours, a time of true technological revolution, is not a time for exultation. It is not a time for despair, either. It is a time for work and for responsibility."

From the presidential address to the Society for the History of Technology, presented in San Francisco.

5

Management in the Big Organizations

1967

It is an open question whether mankind will be around long enough for the historians to go to work on the twentieth century. But if and when they do, 100 or 200 years hence, they will surely put into the center of their attempt to understand this crazy time of ours something that we generally pay very little attention to. They are likely to see as a center of this century of ours the emergence of the large-scale organization as our organ for the accomplishment of practically every single social job of an advanced society.

If you go back to, let's say, the year before World War I started, 1913–1914, well within living memory, you would find a society in which the large organization was unknown by most people. Most people had no contact with it, had never seen one, had only been aware of it the way one hears of monsters, dragons, sea serpents, and other curiosities that may or may not really exist.

The YMCA in the United States today spends more money annually than the total budget of the United States before World War I. Your budget is well over $200 million, and you are not a large organization by our modern standards. I don't know how many people realize that the army of tiny little Israel, with two and one-half million people that just defeated the Arabs, packs

20 times or more firepower than the Imperial German Army packed in 1914 when it almost overran Europe. Each Israeli soldier has at his disposal almost 2,000 times the firepower of the Prussian soldier of 1914. There were then no universities in the whole world that had as many as 5,000 students. The two that came close to it, Berlin and Tokyo, were considered by all experts of that time to be so big as to be totally unmanageable.

In 1911, as I think most of you know, the U.S. Supreme Court split the largest business of that time, the Standard Oil Trust, into 14 pieces. By 1940, every one of those 14 daughters was larger than the parent had been 30 years earlier by every yardstick: employees, capital, sales. And yet only three of these Standard Oil Companies were major oil companies. The remaining 11 were mostly quite small and unimportant; yet every one of them was larger than the "octopus" that had frightened our grandparents.

But much more important than the scaling up in size is the fact that the large organization is not just confined in one sphere. It is a general phenomena. What we mean by a "small business" would have struck our great grandparents as unmanageably large—300 to 400 employees. Nobody would have known what to do with them in 1880, and as late as 1914 most activities were carried out in family-size undertakings or in very small partnerships. Dickens's picture of a business consisting of the boss, with a confidential clerk who every once in a while would run out for tea or beer, was still the picture of 1914 by and large.

And so it goes, whether you talk of research, business or government, of health care or education, or of volunteer agencies like the YMCA. In every country you could have moved the entire government of 1914—federal, state, and local—into a single one of our new government buildings and still have room for a bowling alley and skating rink. This is true of Japan and Germany, of the United States, England, and Australia, and of Russia. It's true also of all other institutions.

Every place we see the emergence of large-scale managed institutions as the center. I am not going to talk today about whether this is good or bad. It's obvious that some things we are very proud of are largely the result of this institutional development. The "education explosion" is one result. Organization is our means for putting knowledge to work. Before the large institutions arose, knowledge was by and large a luxury of which even a rich society could not afford a good deal. For what could the man of knowledge do? There were only the traditional professions that had not changed in 2,000 years—the priesthood, the law, medicine, and teaching. As to the rest, a little knowledge was a dangerous thing. It was at best an ornament, and the sooner you forgot it and started selling bonds, the better off you were. I started to work at age 18 as an apprentice clerk in an export house in 1927, 40 years ago. The one thing my then bosses knew was that I had stayed in school much too long for a commercial career (and they were right, incidentally). My boss's son had gone to work at age 14. Eighteen was an unthinkably late age for anyone to go to work in the world of commerce. Today a youngster who has only a high school degree is barely employable. We are rapidly moving toward the blessed utopia where you have to have a Ph.D. to be admitted into first grade. Maybe we overdo it, but the fact that we can have work for people of knowledge is a result of organization. This is the primary purpose of organization—its ability to put knowledge to productive work.

You may say this is highly commendable and praiseworthy. But the society of 1914 had its virtues—a society that looked very much like the Kansas prairie, a society on which the highest thing on the horizon was the individual. Sure, there was a little hill over there that looked terribly big: the government. In reality, it was exceedingly small, as witness the fact that of the 48 governors, only six or so held office full time. The remaining 42 kept up their law practice or their real estate office. There simply wasn't enough work to do and certainly not enough pay to be a full-time governor. Perhaps there is something to be said for this simple society.

My point to you is that we don't see as a rule that all our social tastes are these days being discharged in and through large organizations. I am sure, for instance, that when you read the title of my talk today, you thought that I was going to talk about business. But this managed organization is a general phenomenon. We just don't yet see that way.

The only ones to understand our society fully are the "hippies." You may not particularly approve of them (and I am an old-fashioned believer in soap and hot water), but at least they realize that it isn't this organization or that organization. They realize that they are surrounded by organizations—and they are against *all* of them. Philosophical anarchism is a defensible position in theory. The only trouble with it is it never works. This one isn't going to work either. The reaction of the "hippies" is purely negative, and it isn't going to get them any place except into trouble. Still, they at least see reality.

It is not coincidence that the rebellions against the organization of the last few years have been against organizations that nobody had seen before as big bureaucratic machines. I'm thinking of the rebellion of the bishops of the Catholic Church against the Roman bureaucracy at the Vatican Council, which came quite unexpectedly, and the rebellion of the students against the University of California.

Nobody ever thought of those as "institutions" before. It was always big business or big government that was considered the "octopus," depending on whether you are a Democrat or a Republican. But we always saw one institution and believed the rest of society was to be essentially free of them. This is not true anymore.

We have to learn to see the reality of a society in which even the YMCA is a big institution, and a powerful one, and a bureaucratic one by necessity, in which there have to be rules and regulations and executives. For, of course, every one of these institutions is a fiction. You read in the papers that General Electric raised the prices of electric blankets, but in fact some people at GE did this. General Electric by itself can't do anything. Neither can the YMCA, or the University of Nebraska, or the Defense Department, or any other of these institutions. The institution is shorthand for people. In every one of them the effectiveness—indeed, the existence—of these organizations depends on the executives.

They are a very sizable number of people, but they still are a minority—one out of fifty or one out of every hundred people. Their dedication and effectiveness set the basic tone, the basic direction, the basic purpose of the organization. Because our study of these organizations has focused on business or on the government agency, we do not see as yet that there is a common and a new task: the task of the executive. It is a new task only because the number we need is so much larger than any such decision-making group we have ever had. It is a new task because it's a new kind of organization we have never had.

Each of these organizations is concerned with only one small area of human needs, human wants, and human satisfactions. If you compare our present highly pluralist society with any other pluralist society, you will see the difference. We had a pluralist society only a few hundred years back. But then, the various kinds of organizations were all doing the same thing. The king and the duke, the baron and the count, and the abbot down to the yeoman were all landowners. All, in effect, ran total communities, concerned with all community needs. They only differed in size.

We have no one total organization. Every one is fragmented; everyone is partial. One is there for the satisfaction of economic needs, and the other for the satisfaction of health-care needs, and the third one for defense, and so on. This is a very different situation from any we have ever had. And the one thing we can say so far is that all of them depend for their performance on the executive. This very complex society of ours depends on the executive, the manager, the administrator.

What do we need from him? We need several different things.

First, managers must recognize that these organizations exist for a need of ours. They are not an end in themselves. In fact, in themselves, they make no sense whatever. You could not imagine them someplace where there aren't people around. They are servants for a specific, narrow need of society.

The real problem here is not what organizations should be doing, but how they prevent themselves from doing the wrong things. The greatest problem we have here is that every single organization tends to tackle far more things than it could possibly handle. They all splinter themselves. They are all ineffectual because they try to run in 50 directions at once.

Organizations also tend to keep on doing obsolete and resultless tasks. This is the one area where business is way ahead of the rest of us simply because it's got the market test. The Ford Motor Company, we say, abandoned the Edsel. Well, this is polite euphemism. You and I abandoned the Edsel. All the Ford Motor Company did was finally accept the fact when they no longer could conceal it. They tried not to accept it as long as they possibly could. But if you are in a market, there comes a point where you no longer can deny results and their verdicts.

We have government policies around that are infinitely more bankrupt than the Edsel ever was—our relief policy and our farm policy, for instance. But all we do when it becomes obvious that there are no results is to double the money. There is no market test. If we had had a Ministry of Transportation in 1820, a great many of us today would occupy well-paid positions on the staff of the "Institute for Rehabilitation of the Horse." Likewise, when a subject becomes totally and hopelessly obsolete, the university makes a required course out of it.

It is terribly hard for any institution to abandon simply because there is too much emotional investment in yesterday. The less productive the effort, the harder one has to work to squeeze a little result out of it, the more enamored of it do we become. The real problem in the objectives area is therefore how to concentrate and how to abandon yesterday.

The second area in which executives have to perform you might formally call "management." How do we get common effort from a large number of people, each of whom is doing a different job?

When they built the pyramids, they had 60,000 people there. But they had no management problem because all anyone did was to pull on a rope when the supervisor shouted, "One, two, three, hup." They did not have to worry what the workers should do, how they should integrate their efforts, or how to communicate. They were all pulling on the same rope.

But today in all our institutions we have the meteorologist next to the economist, next to the banker, next to the salesman, next to the quality-control engineer. Everyone does different knowledge work, and yet we have to get one result out of all of them.

The next management area is that of the effectiveness of the individual executive himself. His is a different role, a role for which the rules have to be written.

We also face areas of organizational ethics in which we have to learn a great deal. One can't do business, whether as a hospital or as a soap company, without employing people to do the work. One has to be someplace and has to have an impact on a community and its values. The ethical values of an organization are therefore crucial, and we know very little about them.

The relationship of these institutions to each other is also very peculiar. The United States government asks Company X to take over the War on Poverty, and at the same time it's putting the executive of the same company in jail for antitrust violations. Caltech and MIT have more profit-making subsidiaries than Sears Roebuck has stores, but they are "nonprofit." Business corporations are increasingly doing governmental work and community work. This is a very peculiar mixture indeed.

We do not yet know the relationship among these institutions. We do not know the relationship between institutions and society as a whole. We do not yet know the relationship between institutions and the individual.

In many ways, the new capacity to organize and to manage is a great strength. But it is very recent—not even 100 years old. It is also not very common outside of a very small group of people, most of them white (with the exception of the Japanese) and most of them in the Northern Hemisphere. The underdeveloped countries are underdeveloped today mostly because they don't know how to manage—and we don't yet know how to teach them. We do know that this is the lacking ingredient. The moment you can manage, you are no longer underdeveloped. You may still be poor, but you know how to get out of poverty fast.

The new thing that we have developed—or are developing— is a new social structure in which we use our newfound capacity to manage, to build institutions, to discharge social tasks. This enables us to do things that our ancestors would not have dreamed of in every area, whether you talk medicine, education, science, warfare, or economic development. These are great new capacities for doing better. But they also pose challenges. They pose new problems above all to the manager, problems of his own competence and problems of his own values and responsibilities. We are just beginning to go to work on them, and perhaps the most important thing to say is that at least we are beginning to realize that this is the peculiar, the specific characteristic of our society. It is our peculiar, specific problem—and, I also hope, our peculiar and specific opportunity.

From a lecture delivered at a workshop in Estes Park, Colorado, for YMCA managers.

PART IV

1970s

O f all of Peter Drucker's achievements—advising captains of industry and heads of state, coming up with the term "knowledge worker," winning the Presidential Medal of Freedom—the most remarkable may be this: In 1974, his 800-plus-page tome, *Management: Tasks, Responsibilities, Practices*, vaulted past *The Joy of Sex* on the national best-seller list. Many authors would have considered publishing a definitive work such as *Management* the capstone of their career, especially if they had been writing for more than four decades already. Not Drucker. Astonishingly, the 1970s marked not an end for him, but a fresh start of sorts; two-thirds of his 39 books would be published *after* he reached age 65. Drucker would later trace his indefatigability to the 1920s, when he worked as a trainee at a cotton export firm in Hamburg, Germany. Every week, Drucker would escape the drudgery of his job by going to the opera, and it was there that he heard *Falstaff* by the nineteenth-century Italian composer Giuseppe Verdi. "I was totally overwhelmed by it," Drucker recalled. But what impressed him most was when he later discovered that Verdi's masterpiece—"with its gaiety, its zest for life, and its incredible vitality," as Drucker put it—had been written by a man of 80. "All my life as a musician," Verdi declared, "I have striven for perfection. It has always eluded me. I surely had an obligation to make one more try." Drucker said that this vow from Verdi became his "lodestar," helping inspire him to write and write and write.

6

Politics and Economics
of the Environment

1971

I am a very old environmentalist. Way back around 1947 or 1948, when I taught at a small women's college in Vermont [Bennington], I offered what was perhaps the first course in the environment. I did not get a single student then for such a course; nor could I find any reading matter. It seemed a very strange and wildly reactionary notion at that time that we have to make sure of not destroying too much of the natural inheritance of man.

Having been concerned with ecology for a long time, I should be exceedingly pleased by the sudden rush of interest in the environment—to the point where one cannot open any magazine without finding an article on ecology in it. And in a way I am, of course, grateful. It is very nice to see that one was not entirely wrong a long time back.

But I am also rather perturbed. I see an enormous amount of busyness and an enormous amount of headlines and an enormous amount of rhetoric, but the only thing I don't see are results. Maybe I demand too much. But I do not see much progress. I see a lot of money being spent. But I have long ago learned that one does not equate the size of a budget with accomplishment. Money is no substitute for thinking; indeed, to substitute money for thinking always does damage. I see a lot of bills being passed, a lot of conditions being deplored, yet don't see us making much progress in learning how to manage the environment to make this country and this planet livable for human beings.

And so I have been asking myself just these last few years not only what should be done but also what should *not* be done. Why are we making so little progress despite all the tremendous emotion and stir?

The first thing to say is that most of the present advocates of the environment suffer from three major misunderstandings, which inhibit results. The first misunderstanding, and the one that bothers me the most, is that we think that one can live in a riskless universe, that one can somehow deprive human action of risk. To believe that one can be safe is a sheer delusion. The real challenge in the environmental situation is to think through what risks we can afford and what risks are not permissible and where to draw the line, and what price to pay for what degree of insurance.

The second misunderstanding is that somehow profits can pay the costs of managing the environment. Yet we have known for a long time that there is no such thing as profit anyhow; that's an accounting delusion. There are only the costs of the past and the costs of the future. So it is a gross misunderstanding that profits can take care of the environmental bill. The consumer will have to pay it, as in the end he pays for everything, whether through taxes or in the supermarket.

Finally, there is the misunderstanding that it is "greed" that explains the environmental crisis. No, it is largely the desire not to see two out of three children die before they reach age five; for the poor to have enough to eat; and to have access to job and opportunity. The environment is a problem of success. These are the hardest problems. They do not yield to attack by morality; they have nothing to do with it.

We have succeeded in doing things that I don't think anybody would consider the wrong things. No scientist or technologist at the time foresaw that the American and Japanese armies would export the screen window to the four corners of the earth, which is the real secret of the "population explosion." Between 60 and 80 percent of the increased birth rate in the tropical countries is the result of the screen window; and that's hardly sensational technology, by the way. The screen window explains in large part why babies no longer die of fly-borne diarrhea before they reach the age of two. One cannot prophesy. One can only say that success always creates problems.

Another major reason why we are not making much progress in our fight to save the environment is that we go about the job by trying to punish instead of by trying to create incentives. If there is one thing we know, it is that punishments do not work—but incentives do.

We are trying to pretend that the environment can be handled by becoming again children of nature. (You know children of nature today play electronic guitars. Every time I hear an antitechnology ballad sung on an electronic guitar with the latest amplifiers, I kind of wonder.) My generation (including myself) did that too, in the '20s. Yet we did not end up anti-technologically, we ended up with the atom bomb. Perhaps if we had learned more about technology instead of singing romantic "blood and soil" ballads we would have done better.

The environment is probably the toughest technological challenge we have faced. Nobody need apply who is not ab-solutely first rate in science and technology and systems work analysis. Folk singers are not going to solve the environmen-tal crisis. They could not even build a sewage treatment plant. (This is the time, by the way, when one tells a youngster not to fall for the nonsense that we do not need engineers. This is the time to go in for engineering. Eight years from now we will need them badly and are going to be very short of trained technologists.)

But perhaps the greatest single problem we face is that nobody is willing to set priorities in the attack on the crisis of the environment. Nobody is willing to say there are 50 million jobs to be done, yet nobody can do more than one at a time and that is usually hard enough.

What are the things we do first, the things to commit ourselves to, the things to work on until they are licked? Instead, we run off in all directions.

In preparation for this lecture, I took the telephone and called up a friend at the Library of Congress and asked, "How many environmental bills have Congress and the states passed by now?" I expected him to say 60. But his answer was 344. I said, "Are they all funded?" "Yes," he said, "they are all in some budget." I asked, "Are they all staffed?" and he said, "Don't ask silly questions."

We are running off in all directions. Everybody with a little hatchet and a spray gun is attacking huge problems. As a result, we get lots of headlines. And that's all we get. And lots of ulcers, and that's all we get. But we get no results.

I am not saying that I know what the priorities are, though of course I know what *my* priorities would be. My list is not terribly important, but a list is important.

My list, by the way, would be clean air first and clean water next and then the problem of thermal pollution in generating electric power for which we have no technology so far. Finally, I would put the food problem, for we are caught in a dilemma between having millions of children die as a result of a sharp drop in crop yields if we stop using herbicides and pesticides, and doing inevitable ecological and biological damage because the pesticides and herbicides are too potent. In the long run this may be the most tragic problem we face. But so far few people are even working on the problem.

This would be my list. But what matters is that we settle on a list and then organize very scarce resources for work. It is not money that is scarce; it never is. But good people who can really come to grips with enormous tasks like the environment are very scarce. Instead of concentrating on a few big tasks, everybody rushes off every morning in a new direction. The right thing to do is to say instead: Here are our priorities. They are either—like air and water—the problems we understand, at least to the point where we know where to start, or, like electric energy and food production, they are problems where we do not know the answers but know that we need answers urgently so that we can do the environmental job. Let's forget in the meantime about all the other things, or let's relegate them to the Sunday supplement where they are forgotten by Tuesday afternoon.

The lack of priorities is perhaps the most serious matter today. As a result everybody is excited about the environment. But nobody is willing to develop any commitment, any policy, or any real attempt to do something effective except to be self-righteous.

We have to think through what the priorities are for this country. Then we have to think through how to carry them out in such a way that the necessary and badly needed and highly conservative concern for the environment does not degenerate into the real sin of conservatism, namely into a war of the rich against the poor, either at home or abroad.

The poor always suffer the most when things become more expensive. Then the one who has the least gets less. There is no way out of this if costs go up. That the black community considers the environmental excitement an attack on it is no accident; the black poor are right. When they think that the white kids on campus who are now all in favor of "earth" are in effect deserting civil rights, they are right. When air is no longer free so that you have to pay for it, it makes everything more expensive. When water is no longer free because you have to pay for keeping it clean, it makes everything more expensive.

We also have to reconcile the needs of the environment and the need for jobs. Twenty years ago, up in northern New England, where the old paper mill is the mainstay of the small town, everybody in the town was willing—indeed eager—to suffer the smell for the sake of the jobs. Today, perhaps, the decision is not so clear-cut. Tomorrow it is going to be clear-cut again—and, again, the vote will be for the jobs. There is going to be no labor shortage the next 10 years because the babies born during the baby boom are now reaching the labor market.

From now on, for the next 10 years, there will be 50 percent more job seekers on the labor market each year than we have had the last 15 years. So there is going to be no shortage of people. Then people will again think of jobs. We are on a collision course between environment and jobs, and I do not think we can afford it. We will have to think through what risks we are willing to take to maintain jobs for people who otherwise would not have any. For those people in Ticonderoga, north of Albany, New York, there are no other jobs, nor are there in Maine or in West Virginia.

No one knows how much money we are spending today on the environment. But the amount is high—up in the billions and going up rapidly. If there are no results in a few years, we are going to get a terrific backlash and a terrific disillusionment. Many people who are now wildly excited about ecology will then say, "It's only a political racket after all." Then I think the ecology would be in for a very rocky time, and we have enough difficulties without inventing unnecessary ones.

The time has come for those who are really concerned with the environment—and not just concerned with the *excitement* about the environment—to say, "What do we do?" rather than, "What do we say?" Are we facing the imminent doom about which you can read in every Sunday supplement these days? Probably not yet. But it is pretty late. We'd better go to work rather than being satisfied with proclamations. We'd better demand results rather than good intentions. We'd better demand a plan and a thought-through program rather than good vibrations, which are not particularly useful in this enterprise. We'd better insist on concentration and work rather than permit rushing around.

For an old ecologist, it is wonderful not to feel totally alone any more, as I have felt for a long time, and to see all those friends and all the people who share my concern. It is wonderful to see all the people who are in effect truly conservative—for there is no more conservative cause in the most profound sense of the word than the maintenance of the balance between man and his environment and between man and man and between man and his values.

But as an old ecologist I am also getting impatient. It's been a long time. If we don't convert all this heat into light and all this excitement into work, we will, I am afraid, be badly frustrated and soon give up on the environment. Excitement cannot be sustained unless there are results. And so what I am concerned with is not activity but results. What I am concerned with is not what is wrong with the world but what do we have to do to put it right.

From a talk delivered as part of the Claremont Colleges Annual Lecture Series.

7

What We Already Know about American Education Tomorrow

1971

W e all know that the American school is in crisis today. In fact, there are people around who talk about "de-schooling America" and who prophesy a future in which there will be no school at all. This, bluntly, is not going to happen. But there certainly is ahead of us a long period of turbulence and crisis, of rethinking of fundamentals, and of building school systems that will look very different from any we have seen so far.

It is, therefore, important, I submit, to realize that we understand the problem—despite all the rhetoric and emotion around it. We know why the school is in crisis. We already know what American education tomorrow might, or at least should, look like. And we can at least guess at where the new methods and concepts are first going to become practice and accomplishment.

The first thing to say—and it cannot be said too often—is that the school is not in crisis because it is doing worse all of a sudden. The school is in crisis because its role for individual and society has changed so greatly, because it is so much more important than it ever used to be.

The entire school system, in every country, has been based on the assumption that "learning" is an intellectual activity. "Learning," the schools assume, is done in and by a separate organ, "the mind," divorced from, indeed opposed to, "the body" or "the emotions." "Learning," the schools assume, is a separate activity, divorced from, indeed opposed to, "doing." At best, it is a preparation for "doing."

In the Socratic tradition, "learning" had nothing at all to do with "doing"; to connect the two was a vulgar debasing of "learning" and the destruction of "knowledge." And "learning," because it was "preparation," was for the young. The stage in the life cycle in which the human being was deemed sufficiently mature to have attained "rational understanding" but not mature enough to be able to do productive work was the time for "learning." And one stopped learning as soon as one began "doing."

Today we know that learning is a continuing biological process. It begins at conception and ends only at death. And there is no difference at all in the way the infant learns or the adult learns. There is only one learning process.

We further know that "learning" is not an activity of one specific "learning organ"—the mind or the intellect. It is a process in which the whole person is engaged—the hand, the eye, the nervous system, the brain. It is indeed the specific process of living beings, from the most primitive to the highest forms. There is a beginning to life and an end to life. But there is no beginning to learning and no end to learning, though there are sequences to it.

And so "school" as the institution in which one "learns"—while every place else one "does," whether in "play" or in "work"—is becoming untenable. The baby's crib is equally a "learning institution," as is the job or a severe illness. School not only has to adapt to itself the little we know about how human beings learn, it has to change its image of itself as something apart and quite unrelated to the rest of personality and life to something that organizes, heightens, and affirms a central and existential fact of total human life experience. It will have to restructure itself to be part, a crucial part, of "learning" rather than an isolated, superimposed mechanism for "education." And "learning" is lifelong rather than the special limbo for those too old to "play" and too young to "work."

No one can foretell what will happen in the schools this year or next. But we already know reasonably well where we will come out—or at least where we should come out. Seven goals, seven destination points, seven fundamentals of American education tomorrow can already be discerned.

1. Tomorrow's school will be based on the principle of "no rejects." It will be based on the firm assumption that the school can guarantee that every child will reach a minimum—and a high minimum—of accomplishment in the fundamental skills. We no longer can permit ourselves to talk of "dumb" or "lazy" children. In the first place, there is too much at stake to accept that alibi. Secondly, we now know that's all it is, an alibi. It is simply not true. All the evidence we have indicates that even the least well-endowed normal child has more than enough capacity for the acquisition of basic skills.

2. Learning tomorrow, from preschool on to the most advanced adult continuing education, will utilize and put to work the individual's own rhythm, his own learning speed, his own pattern. Traditionally, we had no choice. With 30 or 50 children in the classroom, the teacher had to impose on all of them the same pattern. The lockstep of education was a necessity. This is no longer true. I am not talking of computer-assisted instruction. I do not believe that the task necessarily requires huge machines and a tremendous amount of new technology. But it certainly requires a great deal more by way of tools than we have ever had before. The elementary school and the high school are grossly undercapitalized. We have relied on labor. And that, in turn, has meant that the

teacher's convenience had to be imposed on the entire class, thus making impossible the utilization of the student's own endowment, temperament, characteristics, and abilities. And this we will not permit ourselves any more in the American education of tomorrow. There we will try to the maximum extent possible to utilize the way each child learns best as the way each child learns.

3. American education tomorrow will, at the same time, be achievement-oriented. It will, in effect, demand of itself that it enable each student to acquire excellence in the area for which his own talents and abilities fit him best. This is not doing away with the core skills, whatever they may be. But it is accepting the fact that this is a big and diverse world in which a great many different skills and different talents and different tasks can find useful and productive employment. It is accepting the fact that, thank God, human beings are not alike; each of us has areas of strengths as well as areas of weaknesses. Today's school, in effect, is still the school of the scribes. To be sure, we have added art appreciation and physical education and shop and home economics. But we are really rather contemptuous of everything that is not reading, writing, or arithmetic. Today's school imposes a value system on the human being, which, in effect, eliminates something like three-quarters of human gifts as "irrelevant." This is not only inhuman in the most literal sense of the word. It is not only stupid. It is also incompatible with the realities of our economy and our society. We need people who are crafts-men in thousands of areas. We will expect the school to be achievement oriented. We will expect it to try to find the real strengths of the students, to challenge them, and to make them productive.

4. In its methods the school of tomorrow will be neither "be-haviorist" nor "cognitive," neither "child-centered" nor "dis-

cipline-centered." It will be eclectic. Indeed, it is increasingly becoming clear that these old—very, very old—controversies have been sham battles all along. To learn anything, we need the behaviorist triad of practice-reinforcement-feedback. Otherwise, whatever we try to learn will never get lodged in the long memory and will never become learned. But to do anything with teaming, we need purpose, decision, values, understanding—the "cognitive" categories. Otherwise, "learning" is "behavior" rather than "information," let alone "knowledge." It is "activity" rather than "action." We also know now that it is always the individual who learns; all learning is "child-centered." But it is also something that is being learned; all learning is "discipline-centered." The problem does not lie in this dichotomy of old. It lies in what the right disciplines are—that is, what school tries to accomplish. And it lies in the sequencing of disciplines to satisfy both the learning pattern of the learner and the learning logic of the subject matter. Crawling comes before walking both in terms of bone and muscle development and in terms of equilibrium mechanics.

5. To move to an entirely different area: Tomorrow's school—whether kindergarten, university or continuing education—has to be integrated into the community and to be an integrator of the community. A great deal can be said against the small college of the mid-nineteenth century with its rigid curriculum aimed essentially at training ministers in Latin, Greek, Hebrew, and a little arithmetic; with its narrow religious blinkers; and with its authoritarian structure in which all power rested in a president appointed, as a rule, from the outside by a board dominated by a religious denomination. But one thing can be said for it. It was part of its community—whether the community was the Methodists or the Baptists or the Congregationalists. The modern university, which replaced it between 1860 and 1900—and which has

become completely triumphant in the last 30 years—may be intellectually much richer, much freer, much more rewarding. But it is no community and it has no community. The students of 1870 complained bitterly about the thin gruel that was offered to them as intellectual nourishment and about the stifling bigotry under which they had to live. But not one of them felt "alienated." Not one of them felt without a home, without roots, without family. In fact, they felt far too much "restrained" by a college that, in effect, considered itself the father and mother of the student. American education tomorrow will have to think through who its constituents are. It will have to learn to establish relations with them. It will have to learn, above all, to get across to them what each constituency can and should expect from the school and what the school can and should expect from each constituency.

6. One way or another, American education today will be held accountable for performance. I do not know how one measures "performance" in education. The reason why I do not know this is that one first has to know what the objectives and goals are before one knows what one should measure. If you tell me that the first job, let us say, of an elementary school is to have the children learn to read, I can measure performance, and very easily. If you then, however, add that you want to socialize children—that is, to make civilized human beings out of them; if you then talk of the development of the whole person; and if you add on to this preparation for employment and making a living, you make it impossible for anyone to measure. In other words, the school will be expected to think through objectives and goals, to get them accepted, and then to hold itself accountable for them. If the school does not take on this responsibility, standards of measurement will be imposed from the outside. The educators will then protest violently that these are the wrong standards

and the wrong measurements—and they are most likely to be right. But they will only have themselves to blame. One way or another American education tomorrow will be held accountable and should be held accountable.

7. And finally, the most important change perhaps: American education tomorrow will no longer assume that one stops learning when one starts working. It will no longer assume that one learns when one is too young to do anything else, and especially too young to work. It will no longer assume that learning stops when living begins. On the contrary, it will assume the opposite: Learning is lifelong. And the most important learning, the most important true education, is the continuing education of adults who already have a high degree of formal education and considerable achievement and success in their own work and life. By tomorrow, we will know that the most important periods of learning are probably the ones that were not considered the "normal" learning age—the preschool years, the years of the infant; and the postschool years, the years of the adult. And that, in turn, is bound to have a profound impact on the structure, the curriculum, the methods, and the position of traditional education. We will again return to the stage before the "educational explosion" of the last 100 years, the stage when most people were expected to learn as part of their normal life rather than as something separate from life, isolated from it, and set apart. Only while before, the nineteenth-century learning was almost entirely outside of school, school now is going to be part of life, part of the ongoing, the continuing, the normal everyday experience of the adult, and especially of the highly educated adult.

From the William T. Beadles Lecture for the American College of Life Underwriters.

8

Claremont Address

———————

1974

Ladies and gentlemen, I am very pleased to be here today, and I'm very pleased and proud and happy to be a member of the Claremont Graduate School community where I have been now for three very happy years. You asked me today to talk about management and what is ahead for it. Perhaps the best way to start might be to say that for the last maybe 25 years, the whole world has been in a management boom.

That's what the Japanese call it. Until 30-odd years ago, management was a fairly hidden and esoteric concern of a few people here, there, and yonder. In fact, most managers didn't know that what they were practicing was management. And between you and me, most didn't. What was the very small esoteric concern became front-page news. When I first was ordered to be interested in management I had no such intention until the colonel who commanded me called me in and said, "As of tomorrow you are a management consultant." I said, "Sir, what is a management consultant?" And he said, "Young man, don't be impertinent." Which simply means he didn't know, either.

So I had to learn management overnight. It was very easy because the entire literature on general management at that time was a small bookshelf of six to eight books and some articles. Today I think we publish about a thousand books annually that are indexed by the librarians as general management. That gives

you some idea of the boom and maybe also tells you that inflation didn't just begin last year.

But the management boom is over, and incidentally high
time, too. Like all booms, it lasted too long. Now we face the age
of management performance. For the last 25 years there have
been a lot of promises and a lot of good work, but I think the
time when we will have to prove that we have learned something
in management is just ahead. But also the time when we will
again have to learn new things because the management boom
was very largely fueled by knowledge and experience that had
been garnered in the long years when management was essentially obscure and was being worked at by a very small number of
people in businesses and in a few academic environments. They
provided the capital on which we have been living in management fairly lavishly these last 25 years, and now we will have to
begin to get new knowledge, attacking new challenges.

I'm only going to look at some of the things that I think
institutions today, let alone those who are coming into management tomorrow, will have to concern themselves with. We are
at the end of what is the longest period of economic continuity
in modern western history—almost 30 years since the end of
World War II in which essentially the lineaments didn't change
much. This is longer than at any time before. That era is clearly
at an end. So the manager will have to learn to tackle economic
challenges, which he doesn't yet know about. And incidentally,
bluntly, I am very much concerned at the total lack of preparation, and that's a deplorable state of economics, particularly for
people who will have to perform. I am very depressed by the fact
that my students don't know anything, and what they know is
not relevant. I think we will have to learn economics, economic
structure, and economic dynamics, very much the hard way
again. The manager will have to learn it because the academi-
cians aren't going to help you much. So he will have to learn.

We will again, I think, have to learn to innovate, for we are at the end of a period of technological continuity. I know this sounds very strange. All of us have been led to believe that we have been living in an age of rapid technological change. And then you look at the facts, and it just ain't so. Until very recently, there was no industry around for which the basic technological foundations had not been laid before World War I. The computer, you might say, was the first one of which this isn't true. Technologically we have been modifying, we have been extending, we have been adding on, but we have not been innovating.

In social innovation, which in many ways is far more important than technological, we haven't been doing much either. We have been extending and we have been taking fairly well known things to the four corners of the earth, but we have not greatly added. We are facing a period which is far more likely to be like that heroic age of innovation from about the Civil War period to the First World War. The period began with the aniline dyes and the first practical dynamo in 1856, and ended with the electron tube in 1911. A technological innovation came out on average every 14 to 17 months, leading almost immediately to new businesses and new industries. And incidentally, at the risk of shooting down a favorite balloon, there is no evidence that technology is being diffused any faster today than at any time in the past; in fact, there's a lot of evidence that it is much slower. Within nine weeks after Edison demonstrated the first electric lightbulb, they sold shares in electric lightbulb companies in England. And delivered lightbulbs. They didn't light anything, but within the space of a year they actually had installations in Europe. The same was true of the telephone. Things just don't travel today quite that fast. It's only that they get a great deal more publicity; that is the only real difference.

Now, I think we face a time when major innovations are likely to come, brought about by energy crises, resource problems, but also by new knowledge, which has been accumulating over the last 30 years in physics and chemistry and biology, and information theory, all of which has yet to produce technology. In the social scene, we probably need even more innovation for the big city, for the environmental problem, what have you. So I think managers will have to learn to be both managers to husband what we already know and understand, as well as innovators to bring about and make effective and productive what we don't yet know and don't understand.

At the same time, the next few years are years in which the unspoken and passive assumptions most of us still have with respect to managing work and worker will be challenged. We face demographic shifts of great magnitude, which you can see even more closely outside of this country. Mexico in the next 10 years will have to find jobs each year for three times as many young people entering the labor force than it ever found in any year of its history. Most of them will not be highly educated or trained, but better educated than any previous generation. The same is true throughout Latin America, Southeast Asia, and to a lesser degree in the developed countries.

We are past the population explosion, but we are now facing the effects thereof, particularly the effects of the tremendous drop in infant mortality in the developing countries. In 1938, the last year for which we have any figures that mean anything, four out of five babies born did not reach age 18 and three out of five did not reach age five. Now, three or four out of every five reach adulthood. This tremendous achievement is presenting us with a short-term but tremendous problem for which, incidentally, neither capitalists nor communists have any answer because they've never faced it before.

At the same time, the more important development, perhaps, is that the composition of the labor force is changing. In this country now about half of the young people coming into the labor force have gone to school beyond high school. They have learned very much. But even more, they have changed expectations.

First, they expect management to be rational. They expect management to behave the way they have been told management behaves. Now you and I, particularly the older ones of us in this group, know that this is sheer delusion. But they expect that there is a way to make decisions—and it's more than just saying, "Do this because I tell you so." That there is some thinking ahead, that there is some rhyme or reason behind what management does. They expect it and, by golly, they're going to get it. Because don't forget: They're going to survive us. They expect that what they have learned will be put to use. They expect to make a contribution and to earn their keep. All the things that we have preached to them, they have swallowed. That may be very stupid of them, but young people do believe what parents and teachers tell them. And we have told them to expect rationality from management. We have told them to expect challenge. We have told them to expect responsibility. And they expect it. Above all, we will have to learn to put these tremendous energies to work. I am frankly not yet seeing any place where this is even practicable. But I think we owe it to ourselves to do so.

Now, at the same time, we also face a challenge that a good many of us 25 years ago thought we had licked: the challenge of productivity.

The world today is threatened by an inflation that nobody can control and which is probably the worst social poison imaginable. It dissolves the bond of community and sets class against class. And in every one of the 30 inflationary periods since the first one, which was in the sixteenth century, the result has been a revolt of the middle class against the establishment, to use modern terms. They feel a bitter betrayal, real bitter; this one is no exception.

And the only answer to it is productivity. When I say productivity I am not talking productivity of labor alone, I am talking productivity of all wealth-producing factors. The productivity of capital may be more important, and it's been going down the last few years.

We also have to make knowledge work productive, including the work of the manager.

I am going to be blunt and say I see very little evidence that knowledge work has become more productive, whether you are speaking of the teacher or the hospital or the government agency or most industrial business managers. Of course, one problem is that we don't know how to define productivity and knowledge work. You can't just measure it the way you measure the number of pairs of shoes that come down the line because there are few things as unproductive and as little pleasing to God or man as an engineering department that with great elegance and precision and dispatch and industry designs the wrong product. So productivity is not easy to define for knowledge work. But we will have to manage it. Without it, we will become the victim of expectations.

I've been talking about specifics. And I really shouldn't. I really should be talking about something far more important and far more pervasive. When some of us in this room here were born, the number of people in the workforce of this or any other developed country who worked for organizations was so small that the census barely paid attention. The great majority of people, of course, were still on the land. Or they had been on the land only a few years earlier—1900, 1895, or so. And there were plenty of people who were employed, but they worked for a master, either as a butcher's boy or as domestic servants or as journeymen in a small craft shop. And the number of people who worked for an organization was a very small and mostly industrial proletariat out of sight of polite society, by and large. Today, eight out of ten work for an organization where there is no master, where even the top man is just another hired hand. And as the events of a few years in the universities made very clear, you can always get rid of a top man if he is a hired hand. Nothing proved to be more fragile than a university president, as you may remember. There is no answer anymore. For the first time in history, this is a society without masters. There are only fellow employees.

From a lecture delivered at Claremont Graduate School (currently known as Claremont Graduate University).

9

Structural Changes in the World Economy and Society as They Affect American Business

1977

My topic is "Structural Changes in the World Economy," and I perhaps best begin by saying that contrary to what most of us believe, the present kind of transition period is an old and very familiar story. Every 50 years or so, since something you might call a modern economy first emerged around 1700, there has been a "go-go decade" in which there seemed to be no limit to growth: 1720, 1770, the 1830s, and the 1870s.

One began in the early 1900s, which was aborted in Europe by World War I and in this country it continued to 1929. And now it occurred again in the 1960s and the early 1970s. And these rather giddy periods are always followed by a pretty massive hangover in which everybody believes that growth has come to an end forever. Let me also say that everybody during every one of those hangover periods believed that we were going to run out of materials. This is the third time in my life that I've heard this, and by now I don't believe it anymore. And frankly there is no reason to believe it. This is one of the normal symptoms of this particular hangover. Every time so far this prediction has then been disproven pretty fast.

Growth continues. In fact, it is usually not even interrupted. But it shifts to new foundations. The same thing is happening already. I therefore would like to talk today about some of the new things you don't find in the headlines that are likely to be more important than the things you do find there. The headlines have a tendency to be focused on the events of yesterday. One cannot write the headlines for tomorrow. And yet the only important ones are the headlines of tomorrow.

And so let me say the most important structural change is something very few people pay any attention to—the great change in population. Let me say for those of you in this room who are businessmen or business students, for instance, that you would have made grievous mistakes the last few years if you had based your business decisions on the unemployment figure. This is the only recession in recorded history in which total employment in all categories, including black teenagers in the inner-city ghetto, went up month after month. There were only three months in which it didn't increase in the last three years. Unemployment also looked very high, and may even have been quite high, though frankly I have my doubts. If you had made business decisions on the unemployment figures, you would have expected people to buy small cars, and that's why GM made its first marketing mistake, because it looked at unemployment figures but didn't understand population dynamics.

One makes decisions by looking in this economy at three labor figures. One is the number of male heads of households out of work. That is still the single most important figure for labor supply, despite the tremendous rush of women into the labor force. The other one is the total number of people employed, which, by the way, is higher now than it has ever been in American history except the last three months of World War II. Only then do you look at total employment; that is primarily a political figure, not an economic one. But if you look at only one of these three figures, you are going to make serious mistakes, and most of my friends have done so, because they did not understand that the population structure is changing drastically.

In all the developed countries of the Free World, from Japan to West Germany, there was after World War II a baby boom of varying lengths and varying intensities—something totally unprecedented. After World War II in this country, the number of children born jumped almost 50 percent in four years. Following the baby boom in all of these countries, there has been a baby bust beginning in 1960–1961, again unprecedented, in which the number of births dropped 25 percent. It has not yet gone up even though everybody, beginning with myself, had predicted it must. And so we had a very short period in which we had a very large number of young people entering the labor force.

Anybody who looked at population figures in the last year of Mr. Eisenhower could predict that we would have a youth decade. What form it would take, you couldn't predict. But the center of gravity of the American population, that with an age cohort that is both the largest and the rapidly growing one, was age 39 in 1959. Five years later, when Lyndon Johnson had become president, it was age 17. No such swing has ever occurred before in peacetime. It had to have consequences.

Actually, there was nothing really different that happened. The kids behaved the way teenagers behave normally—except it suddenly mattered, whereas when they did it in the '40s it didn't matter because they were not the center of population gravity. And just at the time when such august people as [legal and social scholar] Charles Reich of Yale predicted the "Greening of America" it was over, simply because by that time the age of the center of gravity of the population was already beginning to move up very fast. It is now already at the age of 27 or 28. Young adults are the center of gravity. They are the largest and most rapidly growing group because our birth rate collapsed in

1960–1961. Next year, the number of 17-year-olds will be 20 percent lower than it is today, and it will continue to decline for about five years.

The most rapidly growing age group in our population today is older people, people over 65—in part because so many reach that age, in part because those that reach it keep on living. You may wonder why we have age 65 as retirement age. You know the Good Lord did not pronounce it. We invented it in 1919 when the first large retirement fund was instituted. The railroad brotherhoods didn't much want to pay pensions, and so they asked their actuaries, "What is the age which we should set so that we won't really have ever to pay a pension?" And the actuaries came back and said 65, and that's how we got it.

It was purely arbitrary. And today, almost everybody who survives childhood will reach age 65—that is, about 17 out of every 20 pensioners will. Most of them will be in reasonable shape not just because our health has improved but because demands have changed. Let me say in this whole room there isn't a single person who couldn't keep on doing whatever he or she is now doing, if, for instance, at age 65 you had a stiff knee with some arthritis in it from an old skiing injury. It wouldn't bother you in the least. But grandfather who had to go out and weed the potato patch couldn't have done it. It isn't only that we are so much healthier; today's jobs are so much less demanding. Occasionally, I suspect that jobs are not just physically but mentally less demanding as well, and so this is a great change.

In all developed countries of the free world, the support of old people will increasingly be the first charge on economy and society. This is the new population structure. The implications are enormous. They change our whole social and economic situation.

Another implication of the changes in population structure is that we will face an increasing shortage of traditional labor in this country. We will barely have enough labor for manual and low-skill clerical work to do the jobs we cannot farm out. You know the streets of Salt Lake City or of Logan have to be cleaned and the trash has to be picked up. You can't contract it out to a developing country, and the bedpans in the hospital have to be emptied here. But everything else we will increasingly find hard to do, not only because the numbers are not there but because so much of the labor supply is not available for unskilled jobs. Like you in this room, most young people sit on their backsides so long that they are no longer qualified for honest work. That's not what you go to a university for; the main purpose is that you come out as a cost accountant four years later and never do an honest day's work again. And this, incidentally, also means that we will have to learn to use older people and use part-time people.

Our largest single reservoir of labor is older women. For that purpose an older woman is defined as somebody whose youngest child is in third grade and therefore no longer comes home for lunch. This is a most important social watershed in America. The mother is suddenly emancipated but also lonely with no one to talk to but the appliances, and then she goes to work. So we will have to learn to use this social watershed productively.

If you look at the developing world, its population dynamics are almost the opposite of ours. There, the increase in life expectancy has barely begun. Average life expectancy in India is still well below 40.

In every one of these countries, the birth rate has been going down very fast, at a faster rate than in the West, but infant mortality rates have gone down even faster. In Mexico today, the birth rate is about 30 percent below what it was in 1938. The infant mortality rate is 90 percent lower: Of every ten babies born in Mexico in 1938, eight were no longer alive in 1958. Of every ten babies born in Mexico in 1958, eight are alive today. This is one of the greatest swings in the history of mankind, and it's typical.

By 1990, the population explosion will be over in the developing countries. Birth rates and infant morality rates will be in balance because birth rates are still going down very fast, and infant mortality rates are no longer going down at all or very little. In another 15 to 20 years, at the latest, they will have established very much our kind of population balance or the balance we had in 1920, perhaps.

But for another 10 or 15 years the major problem of the developing countries will be to find jobs for young people who are not particularly highly trained or highly schooled. But they do have a great deal more training and more schooling than their parents had, and what is much more important, their parents were in the back country, in some God-forsaken pueblo in the hills. If they made any trouble, four rural policemen were sent with submachine guns, and that was the end of it. Now the kids can hop the tailgate of a truck and, four hours later, arrive in a large city. The sleepy provincial towns, which you will still find described in travel books on Mexico written in 1939, now have a 1.5 million people: Guadalajara, Puebla, San Miguel Allende, Oaxaca, are all very large cities now. Their slums are not the ideal human habitat, but they are better than what the people left behind in the pueblo. They have a better diet, more chance of education, even better housing, and the chance of a job that makes the appeal to go to the city irresistible. And these kids, while not particularly well trained, are available. And the only way the developing countries can avoid real catastrophe and social convulsions is to provide jobs for these young people. And almost none of them have enough of a domestic market. Only Brazil perhaps. Perhaps India. The rest can hope to find jobs only if there are jobs for export to the markets of the developed world.

And so the central economic problem of the next 15 years will be to put together our need for labor and their need for jobs in what I, for lack of a better name, call "production sharing."

What it means you see when you look at handheld electronic semiconductors, which are made in two places in the world: Dallas and San Francisco. And about 70 percent of those chips are exported. The steel case then usually comes from India because the Russians built the world's largest white elephant there. They built a beautiful rolling mill in India with two million tons rolling capacity, the largest rolling mill in the world for an automobile industry. But they forgot to build the automobile industry. That is called central planning. And so the Indians have all that sheet steel available. The chips are put into the casing anyplace between Morocco to Taiwan. And then a Japanese trading company puts its brand name on it—that's the only thing Japanese about it, by the way. And now tell me: is that an American export or an American import? We buy back about one of every five of the chips we send abroad; the other 80 percent are sold all over the world. But we pay for those calculators we buy back. We are the largest calculator market. But is the calculator an export or an import?

Or take the shoes you and I are wearing. The hides come from this country because we are the largest producer of cows, and the hide is a by-product of the cow. It's being tanned increasingly in Brazil. We have almost no tanning labor; we couldn't tan it here. Then some of those tanned hides go to Haiti where they are being made into uppers, and some are sent to the British Virgin Islands where they are made into soles. Later the shoes are assembled in Puerto Rico and sold in Logan. Where does the shoe come from? That's production sharing. And that is, on the one hand, the great hope we have and, on the other hand, the great problem. The number of shoe workers who are being displaced by this in this country is very small, 65,000. But they are all in three congressional districts. All three of them are swing districts that can go either way and are therefore very visible and very potent. The tension between an economy to which national economic terms no longer apply and a policy that has to be national is going to increase and increase.

From a speech delivered as part of the George S. Eccles Distinguished Lecture Series at Utah State University.

PART V

1980s

Drucker purists would probably cite his 1985 book *Innovation and Entrepreneurship* as the decade's publishing highlight. But two other titles truly stand out: *The Last of All Possible Worlds* and *The Temptation to Do Good*. For these are novels—testaments to the fact that Drucker saw himself, first and foremost, as a writer (more than as a professor or a consultant or a "management guru," a label he loathed). These works of fiction also underscore Drucker's notion that "management is a liberal art," and, as such, its practice should be informed by lessons of history, sociology, theology, psychology, literature, and more. Drucker himself was a polymath, as likely to read Jane Austen as Joseph Schumpeter, and he systematically drew on all of the branches of learning that he could. "Every three or four years I pick a new subject," he explained. "It may be Japanese art; it may be economics. Three years of study are by no means enough to master a subject, but they are enough to understand it. So for more than 60 years I have kept on studying one subject at a time. That not only has given me a substantial fund of knowledge. It has also forced me to be open to new disciplines and new approaches and new methods—for every one of the subjects I have studied makes different assumptions and employs a different methodology." Certainly, Drucker's keen grasp of history fed his anger about what he viewed as a most unfortunate hallmark of the '80s: escalating corporate greed. He railed against king-size CEO pay. And he excoriated hostile takeover artists and Wall Street traders whose short-term mindset was anything but Drucker-like; he called them "Balkan peasants stealing each other's sheep" and "pigs gorging at the trough."

10

Managing the Increasing Complexity of Large Organizations

1981

If you look at the history of political theory—and basically when we talk organizational structure we are talking governance and political theory—there are two strands in the Western tradition. One is the constitutionalist, which basically says, "What are the right laws so that even mediocre people can function and so that the evildoers are at least confined?" The other one, which went by the name of the "education of the Christian prince" and also goes back to the Greeks and even earlier, says, "How do we form the rulers so that even if there are turbulent times and the rules aren't clear, we get the best there is, and we get virtue and leadership into the system?"

In the last 30 years, we have emphasized the constitutional approach. Let me say that this is normal in this country, where business basically started out taking its structural concepts from the American Constitution. If you look at our organizational theory, it is tremendously influenced by the Constitution, for better or worse. I'd say largely for better because at least it preaches the need to think through the limitations of power. At the same time, we have had some approaches that are opposite—that start out with, "How do we form people?"

Oh, some of you may be old enough to remember that I once was considered a pioneer of human relations, which was an attempt to offset somewhat the constitutionalist approach with an approach on the formation of people. And there is organization development. But let's face it. Those two things haven't worked. They have been minor corrections. And now we will have to look at the formation of people very seriously, simply because for some of the problems we have to solve there is no other way.

Let me give you an example. If you look at multinationals today, they are mostly nineteenth century in their structure, with a parent company and with subsidiaries that manufacture the same products for their own home market. But increasingly, you get incestuous relationships in which the specs come out of Detroit, the design comes out of Germany, the body comes out of Brazil, and the transmission out of Mexico—like the Ford Fiesta. Or if you look at IBM office products, resources are organized not in terms of products but in terms of stages of production with labor-intensive work done in one place, with design done in another, with a lot of the technology done where the technologists are.

And let me say that technologists are proving remarkably resistant to migration. Those French specialists prefer to work in a research lab near the Louvre to working in Hoboken. I can't figure it out, but they do. And you can't get them to move or even to go down to Connecticut, and so you have to do the research where the researchers are. It's no longer true as it was in the '50s that researchers are so badly paid in Germany or Austria or Japan that they'll only too gladly take that job in Peoria. They don't anymore. And so you will have to think through how you organize and integrate not components but stages. The product is then sold where the customers are, which is likely to be in developed countries. And so that subsidiary you have in France is not a traditional one.

But even more difficult is the subsidiary in Colombia, where, if you are a pharmaceutical company, Colombia is a developed market. In fact, the only industry for which developing countries are fully developed markets is the pharmaceutical for the simple reason that pharmacy is the only part of modern health care a very poor country can really afford. It's the cheapest part, and it does 60 percent of the job. And so Colombia spends proportionally more per capita on prescription drugs than most developed countries, and yet it's a small market because of the small urban population—roughly similar to one good sales district in a developed country, let's say Manchester or Kansas City.

And yet that head of your subsidiary there has to be a distinguished man because he will matter a great deal. So he probably is the most distinguished medical administrator, former dean of the medical school, and a minister of affairs. How does he relate to the top? He has to be an equal because he'll negotiate with the government there now, with the Catholic nun who buys drugs for Mercy Hospital. You'll need his input. He's a very distinguished man; very few of that caliber could you get into your own organization. How do you structure him? And so you have all kinds of new complexities, which make the simple, traditional structure very hard. Then one has to say, "First, we need new structural principles." The answer to it is, "We ain't got none. We have patchwork."

We had in the history of organization two very simple principles. One is from [French mining engineer and early twentieth-century management theorist] Henri Fayol, and the other one was what [General Motors Chairman] Alfred Sloan and then I codified as "federal decentralization." And they worked where they worked like a charm, but they have strict requirements and severe limitations.

You know, when I first heard of the Bell telephone system, it was beautifully organized and very simple, a good operating company, and 98 percent of their business was within their territory because in those days 98 percent of all calls and 98 percent of all revenue were local calls. Nobody had heard of computer transmission or what have you. And so, when you look at it today—and you all know the Bell telephone system is desperately trying to reorganize itself into regulated and unregulated and quasi-regulated businesses—you no longer have a local system that's interconnected, a long-distance system with local peripherals. The old organization cannot work and doesn't. And so how do you organize? We don't know the answers; we know patchwork. And we will all have to live with things that quite clearly are full of friction and present problems.

We've tried to build our organizations as close to mechanical models as possible because it is simple. [Scientific management pioneers] Frederick Taylor and Henri Fayol both assumed that you know what you are doing. You know, a coal mine mines coal. It's obvious, isn't it? Well, you are now in a period in which the real challenge is to decide what you are doing in the context of technological change or market change.

The one axis of organization that you'll say you need is a skeleton. And all of you know a land animal that is more than six inches tall needs a skeleton; it can't be held together by heart and skin anymore. The organization chart, with its lines of authority and its reporting, is a skeleton. Now, we always have some problems with that. If you have a divisional structure, the relationship between your corporate comptroller and your divisional comptroller is not a simple one and can't be decided one way or another. You all know that when you get to technology, it doesn't work if you have coordinating groups, and it doesn't work any other way.

Yet how do we organize the new within the old? In fact, can we organize it? If you look at the last 30 years, the obstacles to entrepreneurship were exceedingly high in terms of the tax laws, in terms of our credit structure. Now, we are not as bad as the Japanese where the better you do in school, the bigger your employer has to be. We don't believe that bigger is better and very big is best, but we've gotten pretty close to it. We are told that the bright ones want to go into small business. That's what they say. But when you look at where they are three years later, they are all with Citibank, and for good reasons. Citibank can afford people who don't earn their keep yet. Citibank can afford that overhead, and that little entrepreneur with $2 million in sales can't. But he also has no time to train anybody. He has to throw them in, and also they learn the wrong things. One has to learn system.

Before you can say what we violate in the system, you have to master it. You can't write free verse until after you have learned to write a sonnet. I once studied composition with one of the most advanced of modern composers [the Austrian] Anton Webern. (I almost became a musician.) And I thought he would let me write the kind of stuff he wrote. And he said, "My dear, Peter, you are taking liberty with the variation form. [Joseph] Haydn gets it after 30 years. First of all, you will never be a Haydn, and you have been at it 30 days." And I had to learn to write the orthodox variation. And then, after I had done that for a year badly, he said, "Now, maybe you can take one liberty, but be careful." And, I brought it in, and he said, "I was wrong. You aren't ready yet." And he was right.

And, that's why students go to the GEs and the IBMs: not only because they pay better, but also because they have a training program. We have been amazingly effective at having small entrepreneurs, and yet, when you look at the things that need to be done, an enormous amount must come out of existing, large organizations simply because the capital needs, the people needs, and the planning needs are so great.

So, how do you organize your entrepreneurial within the managerial? Again, the answer is largely not structure but people and compensation systems and managing individuals and placing them.

The human relations people made one dreadful mistake, which we now realize. They talked of human nature. That was the reason why we in the human relations movement were totally ineffectual. We talked of a collective called the human being in society. We preached individuals, but we did not really look at them. We didn't manage them. We managed workers, supervisors. One has to do that, but still it explains why we were ineffectual and why the very human beings whom we thought we befriended rejected us. The organization development people believe that structure is an obstacle and an impediment and has to be, if not eliminated, at least bent to the human being. They are equally ineffectual.

The skeleton has to be rigid. One cannot adapt the skeleton to the individual, to people, but one has to fit people as individuals so that they can learn what the individual can learn. We will have to challenge people: "It's your job to think through who has to know and understand what you are trying to do and to make yourself understood. Don't wait for the information specialist; that's futile. It's your job to say who needs to know what you are going to concentrate on and also who depends on you for what. And then to go to that person and say, 'This is what I think you look to me for,' which is the only way to develop relationships."

Every client of mine tells me of the terrible personality problems that we have. Nonsense. Personality problems are very rare in organizations. Organizations have to be very tolerant. Misunderstandings are common. Personality problems are almost unheard of. But what is common is that you don't know what the next fellow is doing because he hasn't told you, and you haven't asked him. And so you assume he must do what to you is obvious, and when he does something else you think he is either stupid or malicious. No, he only marches by his own drummer and hasn't told you what it is and you don't hear it. So, we will have to demand a great deal of responsibility from individuals for making themselves effective in a system.

From a talk delivered at the Peter F. Drucker Symposia at New York University.

11

The Information-Based Organization

1987

It's a great honor to speak under the auspices of the Encyclopædia Britannica, if only because, as some of you know, I've always believed—a very old-fashioned belief—that it is the responsibility of the man of learning and knowledge to make it effective and to disseminate it. The tendency that the less accessible you are, the more you know, is a despicable and very recent heresy and counterproductive. And so I am very greatly honored to talk under the auspices of the oldest and most distinguished disseminator of information and knowledge, which has done so very much over these 200-plus years to further education and self-improvement and information.

And it is only fitting that my topic is the information-based organization. By now, everybody has a computer, and I spent last week up in Boston with my oldest daughter, whose oldest son is now going to college. And I said to him, "Have you picked your typewriter yet?" He gave me a look that would have killed me if I was that typewriter. "I need a mainframe control data computer," he said. He won't get one. His mother's finances don't quite stretch that far. But by now, everybody has a desktop, and so all of you can now put your wife's laundry list on the computer.

We are beginning to drown in information—in data, not information. I began work almost exactly 60 years ago—it'll be 60 years on July 1 since I started as an apprentice clerk in an export house in Hamburg, with a quill pen. And in those days, information was simply—well, there wasn't any. It was a railway timetable, and that was it. Basically, we all learned to manage without information. And now we will have to manage with it.

It's bred in the bones of the human race that the more information, the better—it's quantity that counts. But when information is no longer scarce, believe me, you very soon learn that less is more, and that more is most definitely less. And you learn that quality counts, and that information is something that has to be selected. Information is something that is pertinent to the task that can be converted into knowledge. And knowledge is information in action. One has to learn this.

Let me say, yes, almost any professional learns this in his or her own area. Talk to a good, experienced physician and ask, "What have you really learned in those 25 years since you began to treat patients?" The answer is, "I have learned to decide what information is relevant out of the enormous amount of data I kind of poured into myself in medical school and my internship and residency. And now I know how to recall what I need for this patient." We will learn to do this in organizations.

When you look at our information systems now, though, they are basically totally unselective. You gather as much as you can and distribute it to the largest possible number of people. And that said, you don't get information; you get data. We will have to learn to think through: What information do I need? What is information for me? And this is something we have never done. When I look at my friends in institutions, they still think this is the job of the information specialist. Well, the information specialist knows how to get it, but he hasn't the foggiest notion of what to get, nor can he. And so today you have that peculiar standoff in our organizations between the information specialists and the executives, in which each side basically thinks the other one is—well, not just stupid, that wouldn't be so bad—but malicious and prone to sabotage. And the information specialist is more nearly right than the executive, because it is only the executive who can think through, "What do I need for this job of mine? What is information out of this enormous amount of data? What is relevant?"

Sure, the information specialist may then say, "Look, Mr. Vice President, you can't get it that way. You have to get it some other way." Or he may say, "This I can give you. And this I can give you in the form in which you are used to getting it. And this I can only give you in some other form." Or: "This I can only give you approximately. And this I can't give you at all." That's his job, where it is the job of the executive to think through "What information do I need?"

And now we have to do it because we have big organizations and big information systems. We have to design them and focus them and concentrate them on what we need out of the chaos of facts, the universe of facts, so that it becomes information and our tool.

One could have asked in 1870, "What is the most successful large human organization around?" And the answer would probably have been the British in India. They'd been there for 100 years by then. They ran the subcontinent, but they never had more than 1,000 people and no level of management at all. There was the assistant district commissioner way out in the jungle. He was the nearest English-speaking person 60 miles away, before the telegraph, let alone the railway. And then there was the lieutenant governor in Bombay or Madras or Calcutta, and no one in between except the traveling auditor, traveling inspector. And they did very well, even though they were green kids, 25 or 26 years old, without any training—something the British never believed in, as you know.

Without any preparation they did a reasonable job, because the objective was crystal clear. There were only three things you were supposed to be doing. The first was to maintain law and order. And when the district commissioner came, before he called on that kid, he looked at the homes of the villagers. And if they were padlocked, the kid was relieved of command immediately. It was his job to have such good security in the village, there were no bandits and nobody needed a lock. Secondly, in the land of multiraces, multireligions, his job was to prevent people from killing each other. And he did a better job than the Indian Republic has done, between you and me. In the whole history of British India, fewer people were killed in religious riots between Hindu and Muslims and Hindu and Sikhs and so on than are being killed each year in India today. And his last task was to collect taxes—and in that order, by the way. The idea was that if you can't maintain law and order, you aren't going to get taxes. They knew better than modern American administrations the priorities of government.

And then every Saturday afternoon, that kid sat down and wrote the report directed to the lieutenant general, in which he copied down "What did we expect last week?" from his letter of a week ago. Then he answered, "What did happen? What is the explanation for the things we expected to happen that didn't? And for the things that we didn't expect to happen that did? And what do I expect will happen next week?" And every one of these reports was answered by the lieutenant general or by his political secretary. And so there was clarity of goals and measurable results. You know, you can count the padlocks. Or the ones who get killed in a riot over a cow. The results are carefully quantified. And you can also count taxes. Clear, upward information responsibility.

And if you look at the most successful large organization we have created since we first created the large corporation a hundred years ago, it's the large symphony orchestra. We are moving towards the symphony orchestra, in which you will have many fewer layers of management and many more specialists. The triangle player has no ambition to become a bassoonist, and absolutely none to become first violin. He wants to be a better triangle player, the way our computer people have absolutely no ambition to become marketing vice president, but they want to have a bigger computer. We have many more specialists, and they have to be integrated into the score. And by the way, let me say [Gustav] Mahler taught us how to do it, because Mahler created the modern orchestra when he took over the Vienna Philharmonic. He found in the orchestra's contract that they had to play five evenings, and he said, "No, you are going to be on duty five evenings, but you play four. The fifth evening you sit out in the audience and listen." And somehow we have to force people in our organizations to move where they have to "listen to the music" by putting them on a task force, or by moving them from one specialty to another, or perhaps by making them go back to school.

What we are now seeing is the passing of the giants. I was recently at the University of Michigan, 45,000 students. There is no advantage to that, none whatever. There's nothing you can't do with 8,000 or 12,000. And the liberal arts colleges, probably nothing you can't do with 3,500 today, or even 2,800. Six hundred is too small. There you begin to feel all the things you can't do. And 10,000—no point to it; all you have more layers of vice presidents. At the University of Michigan, the president is leaving, and they wanted me to sit down with the search committee and talk about what to look for in the next one. And I said, "There's only one thing I can tell you: By the year 2010 you're going to have more vice presidents than you have students." And they're going there very fast, simply because they are trying to manage something that is much too large.

I drove by the NYU Medical Center, and my driver asked me why they didn't expand when they had the opportunity to buy up the next block. I happen to know this. It's already too big, basically 2,200 beds. The best hospital is probably about 900—even a teaching hospital. And so you will see small institutions provide the best communication link. The British had 1,000 people to run a subcontinent. You will have concentrated institutions, rather than diversified ones, so that the score is clear. And you will have upward responsibility for information, for objectives, for results, for educating the boss.

And you will see institutions that are groups of specialists. And yet everybody should, theoretically at least, know the music, so that he knows what [French composer Claude] Debussy sounds like and doesn't think only about what the bassoon part is. You must take integrating responsibility for putting yourself into the big picture. Commands go from the top down; information goes from the bottom up. And so we are facing an enormous job of restructuring, which we have just begun.

From a talk given as part of the Britannica Awards, presented by Encyclopædia Britannica to recognize "exceptional excellence in the dissemination of learning for the benefit of mankind."

12

Knowledge Lecture I

1989

I'm always amazed, as a very old political journalist, at how little attention the media and the scholars pay to the truly important events of any period. And if you ask in retrospect, provided this planet survives 200 years hence, "What is the most important event in this century?" you will probably find some people who say the final demise of the utopian creeds with Marxism. And other people may point, and quite rightly so, to those horrible world wars. And there have been very few centuries in which there have been more refugees. And other people will look at the environment. But I think 200 years from now, it's quite likely that the majority consensus will say, "This is the century with the most unprecedented, unexpected changes in the way people work."

If you go back to the beginning of this century—you know, in 1911, the British made the first modern census that asked socioeconomic questions. And domestic servants made up the largest single group in the employed population. Thirty-seven percent of all people made their living working for somebody else. In fact, that famous census defined "lower middle class" as people who do not have more than three servants. And I don't know whether anybody in this room has lately seen a servant. They have become extinct in developed countries. And the interesting thing is they're becoming extinct in developing ones, too. And servants have been the largest employee group since well before recorded history: as slaves, as serfs. And this century began quite conventionally with an enormous array of servants, and it ends with no servants at all.

The other large group—not in Great Britain anymore, but in the rest of the developed world—were farmers. In this country, 1900 was the first census in which farmers were not more than half the American population; they were just 50 percent. When we came out of World War II in this country, more than one-quarter of the population was still farming. In Japan, it was 60 percent—three-fifths. And now, as you know, we are down to 2½ percent in this country, and they're now down to 4 percent in Japan. Incidentally, to me, the most interesting event of the last election was that the American farmer had become a nonperson. Mr. [Michael] Dukakis and Mr. [George Herbert Walker] Bush—remember those two gentlemen?—made one visit apiece to Iowa, gave exactly the same speech, never came back, and never said another word about the farm. Politicians are pretty good at counting heads. And they looked at them and said, "It makes no bit of difference which way those people vote." And it didn't.

But the most important and interesting development is not even the disappearance of those two key work categories. Even more remarkable is that in this century we have seen the meteoric rise and the meteoric fall of the factory worker.

By 1955, about a hundred years after Marx and Engels, the industrial working class had become the dominant group in every developed country, politically and economically. But in the last 30 years, this class that had risen meteorically for a hundred years began to shrink very fast. In this country, in 30 years, it went down from more than one-third of the working population to below one-fifth. In Japan, it's going the same way. And the decline in importance—and I don't necessarily mean quantitative, but qualitative—is even faster. It would have been inconceivable even 25 years ago that in an election you simply wrote off the labor unions. In 1988, neither candidate paid any attention to them. They were simply written off.

I'm not saying that it's final. But if you look in retrospect at capitalism and ask who has been the beneficiary, most of you will answer "the capitalists." And most of you are dead wrong. The great beneficiary of the last 150 years has been the industrial worker. There is nothing in social history comparable to it. And now it's suddenly all over.

The center of gravity is shifting. And, by the way, if you don't understand this, you don't understand all the figures you are getting quoted about income distribution. It's not that the rich are getting richer and the poor are getting poorer. It is that the large middle class, without education and without skill, is no longer growing, but is shrinking fast. And from now on increasingly, in order to earn a middle-class living, you have to have formal schooling.

Believe me, for the last 30 to 40 years, to sit on your rear end and go to school was economically nonrational and counterproductive. The smart thing was to drop out at age 16 and go to work in the steel mill or the automobile factory or the rubber factory, the unionized mass-production factory. And six months later, you would make more money than you had much chance of making by sitting on your rear end and getting a high school degree, let alone a college or a graduate degree. That's over.

I'm going to sit down the day after tomorrow with one of our very large automobile companies, and we are going to spend a morning looking at manpower. And they sent me their internal projections, on which there's a majority opinion and the dissent. And the majority opinion says by the year 2000, assuming the same number of cars to turn out, our employment will be down to no more than one-third of what it is now. And the majority dissent says two-fifths. Well, it's very clear on the basis of their most recent plants, that probably even one-third is high. And this is not automation. This is applying knowledge to the organization of the work.

We are beginning to shift the center of gravity to people who work with knowledge. And don't ask me: Is the tremendous educational expansion of the century the cause, or is it the effect? That's the chicken-and-egg question, and I don't think you can answer it. But it is also clear that even in this country, where manual labor has the highest esteem of any country in the world, people who have sat on their rear ends for 12 or 16 years are not going to get their hands dirty if they can help it.

This is something quite new. In the early 1900s, if you had wiped out the educated people in any society, very few people would have noticed it—very few. They were an ornament. It's only in the 1920s that the majority of American schoolteachers had any training in teaching. The great majority before World War I had finished high school, and that's it. And then they shipped out to Iowa and took over a one-room schoolhouse. And doctors and lawyers in this country, up until the 1920s, by and large, did not yet have to go to school—an apprenticeship was adequate.

This has changed drastically since. And so we have, for the first time, large numbers of people who will make their living putting knowledge to work. And what is perhaps equally unprecedented is that they work in organizations. As late as 1946, you could not get a certificate as a professional engineer in the state of New York, where that title had been invented. You could not get it if you were employed. Engineers were still presumed to work on their own. And in fact, in this country, only two companies hired engineers before World War I—General Electric and the telephone company. And nobody else did until the 1920s.

We lived up in Vermont during World War II and had an excellent small community hospital there. It had no X-ray, no emergency room, no physical therapy, no pathology—nothing. One general practitioner came in Friday night and cut up the cadavers and got five bucks per cadaver. Today, hospitals have four employees per patient. And probably 80 percent of them are not unskilled bottle washers and people who clean the rooms. They are highly trained, highly educated paramedics. The same is true of the university, for better or worse. When I first knew American colleges, nobody had a vice president for development or a placement officer. We had a faculty, period. I'm not saying it was better or worse—it was different.

And so we are at a very big turning point. Yes, you have traditional industrial workers. Yes, you have service workers. But that's not where the growth in employment has been. And that's not where your management problems and challenges are. They are with people who do knowledge work—some very highly skilled, some quite unskilled.

It isn't true that all knowledge work is skilled, and it isn't true that all of it requires a Ph.D. Knowledge work, by definition, is work that you can only do by applying things that can only be learned, or best be learned, in a formal education process. That file clerk of yours is not the most skilled worker, but nobody has ever learned the alphabet by intuition. True mathematicians learn the multiplication table by perception; they see it. The rest of us, if we've learned it at all—and I'm not going to ask for a show of hands—learn it by drill. And that's knowledge work. It has to be acquired in the formal process.

Let me also say that it is knowledge only if it is applied. We in academia think that knowledge is something you learn in the classroom. No. Information—and, we hope, the ability to learn—is acquired in the classroom. What's in our books is erudition. It's when you take it and do something with it, when something happens, that it turns to knowledge.

The oldest debate in Western history is that between Socrates and the sophists about whether knowledge is what changes the person, or knowledge is something that you use for external action. The answer is both. If all you do is have something happen, and nothing happens to you, you haven't really learned. And if something only happens to you, you are not really using the knowledge. And so the question is: How do we take those people we hope have learned something, who have information, and how do we make them effective?

The first thing to say is that we can't make them effective the way we make the hourly worker effective. For one thing, if they are any good, they know a great deal more about their job than the boss does. A hospital administrator would get rid, very fast, of a physical therapist director who didn't know a great deal more about physical therapy than he or she does. This is not a field in which you want dilettantes. The professionals do enough damage. And the same is true of X-ray, and of the medical lab, and of the floor nurse, and of your market researchers, and of your metallurgists, and, I hope, of your salespeople. And so the idea of "do as I tell you to" is nonsense, simply because we don't know what to tell them. *They* have to know.

The next thing to say is that schooling gives people self-confidence and mobility. It gives them horizon. We had a very serious—don't call it "recession"—depression 10 years ago in '81–'82. In the smokestack industries it was a more severe depression than 1932. But unemployment was amazingly low, even in Youngstown. What explains it? The only answer is that the older people had retired, and the younger people had a high school education, which they did not have in the Great Depression. And they had mobility and horizon. Even if that's through a TV set, they have seen the entire world. They have horizon. They don't have to work for you. Sure, they need a paycheck. But let me say they all know that there are lots of jobs out there.

I still hear friends of mine in business talking about loyalty and so on. Don't. Accept the fact that your job has to be of value to the employee. The paycheck is part of it, but only part of it.

Your mission has to be crystal clear. Believe me, very few of your employees are motivated by the idea of making a great deal of money for a leveraged buyout. What is their mission? The demands have to be both clear and very great. There also has to be continual learning and training and standards.

People have no hesitation to change jobs. Every day I get a call from one of my former students who says, "Can I have a recommendation?" And I say, "Why do you want to shift?" And they say, "I have reached about as far as I'll go in this company, and I'm looking." We all know that. We all know that the two growth industries in this country in the last 20 or 30 years are temporary employment agencies and headhunters. People are mobile. Accept the fact that these people are volunteers, and see themselves as volunteers. They see themselves as working there because they want to, not because they have to.

From a lecture delivered at Claremont Graduate School (currently known as Claremont Graduate University).

13

Knowledge Lecture II

1989

The idea for these lectures was conceived about a year and a half ago when I got a telephone call and somebody said, "You don't know me, but I understand that you have done a lot of work in research management." And I said, "Yes, I've probably made more mistakes in research management than most other people, so I'm qualified as an expert."

And that person said, "Three months ago I moved from being a biochemist into being the director of one of the world's largest labs. And for three months I have been studying what my job is. And I've come to the point where I would like to ask you a question: Do you think research can be managed?" And I was near the point of saying, "If you feel you have to ask this question, why don't you go back and be a biochemist again?" And then I thought for a while and said, "The answer is yes—but. It can be managed, but it cannot be managed the way most other things are being managed. It requires very different things." And out of this I started to say it's about time I try to put together what I have learned in many years of seeing good people struggle with this issue. And most of the things I developed to help this particular research director—who, by the way, is still in the job and by now I think enjoys it quite a bit—I applied to knowledge of any kind.

In most of human work, change is very slow. Continuity, both of work and tools, is the rule. When it comes to skills, it is still largely proved that if you get going through that apprenticeship at age 19, you have a very good chance of not having to learn anything new until you retire. But knowledge work is the exception. Change comes very rapidly.

If Socrates the stonemason—that's how he made his living—came and worked for one of those mason yards that make crosses for our cemeteries, believe me, he would not have to learn much. Most of the tools are pretty much the same, except that some of them now have a battery. But if Socrates the philosopher came into one of our philosophy departments today, he would not understand one single word. And I'm not saying that they're better than he was. But they're totally different.

And that is typical. I just finished a few weeks ago reading a history of the library. And the concepts of the library change every 30 or 40 years. One of the great weaknesses of library school is that it teaches the current technology as the permanent one, when all experience shows that what librarians have to learn is how to learn. Or take registered nurses. Over the last 20 or 30 years at least one thing has remained the same: the purpose. But the way the job is done is almost beyond all recognition for a nurse who started in 1950. Knowledge, by definition, changes very fast. And skills, by definition, change very slowly.

This is one of the first things to say in managing. And let me say this was probably my greatest contribution to the research director. After we had worked on it for some time, it hit me that his very big, very famous lab was being basically run statically. We add discoveries, and we add insights, but we don't change the way we work. And once we understood it, we began to realize that to overcome his bottlenecks, his frustrations—not all of them, but some of them—he had to build in continuous feedback and learning. Mostly, this meant sitting down with people and saying, "What have we learned that will force us, or will enable us, will help us, to do things differently?"

As some of you who are in academia know, we don't do this well. We basically assume the old craftsman's assumption about apprenticeship that, once you have gotten your Ph.D., you stop learning and start teaching. Instead, we should be saying, "That's when you start helping others to learn. And that's when you start learning yourself."

A knowledge-based organization has to be an entrepreneurial organization in the sense that it always starts out to make itself obsolete, because that is the characteristic of knowledge. It is not the characteristic of a skill. And I'm not saying that I know how to do it, and I'm not saying that we know how to do it. I'm saying that we're beginning to realize that this makes a tremendous difference.

You've probably heard the story of the old grad who comes back to the fortieth reunion, and the old economics prof is still there. It is May—that's when reunions are held—so this is final exam time. And the grad looks at the final exam and says, "Professor Smithers, these are the same questions you asked us 40 years ago." And Smithers nods and says, "Yes, but the answers are different." We always thought it was a joke. No! This is wisdom. The answers to questions do not remain the same. The answers are different, because we have learned a lot. What we mostly learn is that the answers that gave you an "A+" 40 years ago are the wrong answers. The way we go about solving problems has changed, because that's what you learn. You learn to do a little better, to push back that infinite boundary of ignorance just a bit.

Among the implications of this is that you have to build in organized abandonment. Otherwise, you collapse under the overload. One of the things you learn from working with research organizations is that they become constipated because there's too much. Nobody has unlimited resources. In knowledge work, you have to start out with the need to change, to grow, to do the new, to run very fast with something that opens up. And you can only do that if you make resources available by freeing them from where there are no longer results.

Another thing we need is specialization. Most human beings excel at one thing at most, and not very many excel even at one. And very few people excel at more than one. And I don't think you'll find anybody who excels at three. Yet, at the same time, the computer programmer produces nothing by himself. Results are interdisciplinary.

So, yes, you have to be a specialist. But knowledge has another very peculiar characteristic, which is that the important new advances do not come out of the specialist's discipline. They come from the outside. It makes no difference what you look at. Every one of the things that have transformed the discipline of history, for instance, came from outside—from psychoanalysis and psychology, from economics, from population statistics, from archaeology. These are all things that no historian, during the time I went to school, ever heard of. And if he did, he was told by his prof, "Look, you study to learn how to read a document in the archives. That's difficult enough." The same is true when you look at the forebears of the computer. Very little of it is computer ancestry. Most of it came from other disciplines. Or look at the Mazda Miata, which has its American design center someplace in Orange County. Where did those impulses, those ideas, come from? Not one came out of automotive design. They came from metallurgy, they came from material science, because that car is made with composite materials and plastics and what have you—from all kinds of things that I'm reasonably sure no automotive engineer ever learned in class.

So how do you organize for this—the fact that you must have a discipline as a basis, but you also have to organize an awareness of the meaning of things that happen on the outside? A discipline is a necessary container, but it's temporary—very temporary. And so how do you do it? A good many companies have learned that it isn't enough to have a research director who is a whiz in a certain specialty. You need a technologist who has an awareness of what goes on in other areas. And this is not something we yet know how to do systematically, but it's something we will have to learn.

The last thing to say is that this is work and not good intentions. It's got to be measured. And yet whenever I use that word, people get upset, and they say, "What we do can't be measured."

I don't think I've told you the story of how I got into the management of research. We had just moved from New England to New York, and I was teaching management at NYU. And I had a neighbor who was research director of one of the large pharmaceutical companies, and we discovered that he and I were both enthusiastic but equally incompetent chess players. Nobody wanted to play with us, and so we played together. And one day I came home, and there was this fellow in a great state of agitation. He had waited for me. And I said, "What's the matter, Stanley?" He was always very quiet. And he said, "You know, I've always been complaining to you how totally disorganized our company is, and how we need management. And then I told you about the new president of ours who came in six weeks ago, and how delighted I was with him because he was going to actually start managing the place. Well, he called me in today and said, 'Stanley, I've accepted your proposal, and I'll appoint a budget committee, and everybody will have a budget.' And I said, 'Wonderful!' And he said, 'Stanley, you're going to be chairman of this committee.' And I said, 'Wonderful!' And he said, 'The first budget I want, Stanley, is that of the research department.' And I said, 'Mr. President, what we do in research isn't determined by us, but by what a lot of rats and guinea pigs and white mice and hamsters do when we put substances under their skin or push them down their gullet.' And he said, 'If that is the case, Stanley, please write out your resignation and nominate the brightest hamster. We'll make him research director.'"

It took me six weeks to get across to Stanley what the president had been trying to tell him. And he never quite accepted it. A good many people still feel that way when you say "knowledge work." In other words, knowledge is not, in that sense, quantitative. And so we will have to learn to think through how we measure and how we appraise. And then I think we can begin to focus knowledge work on results.

One result is productivity, which is woefully low—not because people don't work hard, but because we don't know what productivity means. We made the same mistake with manual work—measuring productivity by how much sweat there is, how hard it is, how many hours are being worked, and how unpleasant it is. Before [Frederick] Taylor, the main measurement of productivity was how tired people were when they got home. Well, that's not the measurement of productivity; that's the measurement of incompetence. And we are doing that with knowledge work.

Let me come back to the question I started out with—the question posed by my friend, the research manager, over the telephone a year and a half ago: "Can knowledge be managed?" The answer is: We don't know. But we do know that it has to be managed, and if knowledge is not managed it only costs and doesn't produce. And we know that it has to be managed differently, that you must start out with a few uncommon assumptions, counterintuitive because that's not the way we look at other work. You must start out with the assumption that knowledge changes itself—that more you know, the more it changes. There's the assumption that, by itself, knowledge is an input, and it has to be integrated to become an output. And there's the assumption that knowledge must be concentrated. If you splinter it, you get very little. You get journalism, but not knowledge.

And, finally, we know that there is only one standard for knowledge. Maybe *excellence* is a big word. I hate to use it. But there has to be that kind of self-respect that will not allow you to do shoddy work. And those are some of the things we know about knowledge as a resource. It's always been around, but it's been a very rare resource. And for most human pursuits you didn't need it at all, or very little. But now it's the key resource of a modern developed economy and society, and we are just beginning to learn to manage it.

From a lecture delivered at Claremont Graduate School (currently known as Claremont Graduate University).

14

Knowledge Lecture III

——————

1989

For what we pay people today, we'd better demand some responsibility from them. It's morally corrupting to pay what we pay and then treat them as little boys or girls. The responsibility for their performance is on them—individually and where there is teamwork. We need to go in and say, "What should this organization hold you accountable for over the next 18 months?" Get out of the trap of the annual appraisal that coincides with your budget cycle. It's a good idea to keep them separate. The question is, "What should this organization hold you or this research group of yours or this floor in the department store, this selling floor—what should this organization hold you accountable for by way of contribution and results?"

The first time you ask this, your people will find that this is a very difficult question. They've never thought that way. Most people, believe me, think in terms of work and not in terms of results. Most people say, "I'm always the first one in the office and the last one to go." Well, that may be all right for the night watchman, but for nobody else. What is the contribution?

In some cases, it is very hard to answer. I mean, if anybody were to ask me—and with my dean sitting here, I shouldn't talk about such things—if I were to ask you what should the graduate school hold me accountable for, I would have a very hard time answering it in terms of what happens to students. And yet that's the only place where we have results. But maybe it would be a good idea if I at least were forced to think about it. And when the employee or the employee group comes back to you, don't say "yes" immediately, and don't say "no." It is your right and your duty to approve or not to approve the goals, but think it through.

Let me say that the appraisal needs to start out against preset targets. Now, nine times out of ten, when 18 months later you sit down and look at how this person has performed, you will find that the goals have changed—that three weeks into the year, you called him in and said, "Joe, we have an urgency," or "The plan was based on your obtaining new equipment, and you didn't get it." Still, at least one knows what one deviates from.

The next thing to say is that once the employee has thought through his or her performance and comes to you for a critique, focus on achievement and contribution before you focus on non-performance. The impairments, the bad habits, the areas of ignorance, the things where improvement is needed—they will all come out. You will not have to point them out. You might say, "You may be a little too harsh on yourself here." Or: "This is quite a respectable performance. But in this area, I think you take it a little bit too easy. This is important, and it's not good enough just to get by." And so put the burden of setting objectives and of appraising against them on the individual or the group.

To be clear: There are some areas where you'll have to address a group. For example, it is almost impossible to evaluate individuals in a research department because so much of the work is a team effort. At a pharmaceutical company, the initial stages of pure research are largely individual. But then you get to the stage of developing a class of compounds. And there you have the biochemist and the pharmacologist and the medical people and so on, and you're really talking about a team. In that case, one sits down every three years, perhaps, and says, "What have you contributed that really makes a difference, and what do you plan to contribute that should make a difference?" That isn't the end of it, but you put the responsibility for this on the people.

Somebody asked me about salespeople. I don't know whether you realize it, but salespeople are probably the area where productivity in the American economy has gone down the most. If you adjust for inflation, the saleslady of today in the department store sells about half of what she did 50 or 60 years ago. One reason is that we have loaded her down with all that paperwork. She doesn't serve the customer anymore; she serves the computer.

Meanwhile, the few retail chains in the last few years that have shown outstanding success—the Gap and so on—all follow the same procedure. They go to the salespeople and say, "What should we expect from you?" And then: "What do you need by way of tools and information?" And also: "What impediments do we create?" Most organizations make it difficult for people to perform. And so it is important in managing knowledge people—and not just knowledge people—that we go to them every nine months and say, "What do we do in this organization and in this department, and what do I do as your boss, that helps you do the job you are paid for? And what do we do that hampers you?" And then it's your job to get rid of as many of the impediments as you can.

When you enable people to perform, you can demand performance. And so put as much of the responsibility on people, and keep it on them. And say, "Well, it's no better than you did two years ago. Haven't you learned anything?" And then you will not have much trouble, especially if you accept responsibility for enabling people to do the work they are already paid for.

You know, you could fill this room with books on motivation, and you would still have some 50,000 volumes left over. The trouble is, we don't know how to motivate people—that's why we have to write books about it. But we do know how to quench motivation.

One way is to make it difficult for people to do the work they're already paid for. Another way is to tolerate the poor performer. The poor performer corrupts. If you have the fellow or the woman who is getting old and they've been there 49 years, then okay. "There but for the grace of God go I." But otherwise, accept that the poor performer lets his fellow workers down. You have a duty not to tolerate the poor performer, a duty to the performers. That quenches motivation, when they see that everybody gets the same praise, when we know perfectly well that Jim or Jane hasn't done a lick of work and what they have done is shoddy. That demoralizes.

The third thing is when you misplace people. Spend time on the placement of people. There is nothing worse than the belief that anybody can do every job. That may work on the assembly line, though even there, it's not quite true. But when it comes to knowledge work, you must spend time on placing people where their strengths can become productive. Nothing so motivates as achievement. And nothing so quenches motivation as frustration.

These are all very elementary hygiene rules; nothing new about them. But like most hygiene rules, they're disregarded. And so put that burden of performance on people. And build the idea of people appraising themselves into the work goal, the performance goal, or whatever you call it. And then you don't have to sit in judgment. It's not a good idea for human beings to sit in judgment on others. But then performance will be the judge. And performance will also show where the need is for learning.

In fact, one of the questions to ask when people appraise their own performance is, "What do you need to learn? What do you need to improve? What do you need to change?"

There are also things that people need practice in. They may know the subject theoretically, but haven't done it enough. It's not going back to school; it's doing it more. In other cases, they may have to read up on something. Maybe it's been a long time since they've learned a topic. And maybe it's a good idea to go back and to take out that textbook on cost accounting once again. They're becoming rusty.

Finally, there are areas where people will need to acquire new knowledge and skill. And they'll need to go back to school. Here, the rule of who pays is pretty simple: If it's job-related, you must reimburse it. And let me say the greatest weakness of our nonprofit institutions is that they don't reimburse. They have tremendous resistance against acquiring additional knowledge and skill on the part of their people, and it's stupid. It's very, very shortsighted, and it doesn't save anything. It costs money.

So what do we need? We need emphasis on performance. We need the ability to close down, whether it is a product that's obsolete, a plant that is no longer producing, a business, a division, a skill.

Now, in many cases where skills become obsolete, you can offer people a chance to acquire new skills, but only to a limited extent. In this mobile society of ours, you don't do a colloid chemist any favors by offering him a job when you no longer need colloidal chemistry. He's better off going elsewhere. And we need that freedom to let people go as the business dictates and the technology dictates.

Beginning in the 1930s, the American unions made the job into a property right. And now we see that as a major reason for our lack of competitiveness. It's even worse in Europe. But you know why we have those union rules? Very largely because managements did not realize what was needed.

And if we don't put into our policies the right protection of jobs against arbitrary management action, we will eventually—either through the unions or through the courts—be hit with the wrong ones. The danger of being put into straitjackets, with the equivalent of faculty tenure or union rules or job restrictions, is so very great that this is not the time for management to wait until they're met with a lawsuit. I have learned that managements don't react until they have lost at least one lawsuit.

If we don't do what makes sense—what is productive both for the company and the employees—then I'm afraid that, yes, 20 years from now we'll find ourselves under very severe restrictive and punitive rules. We don't have forever, and maybe being forced by lawsuits to accept the fact that there has been social change is the only way we will ever accept it. Certainly, we are now getting enough lawsuits so that people ought to accept the fact something is happening here. And maybe it's a good idea to move before we are pushed.

From a lecture delivered at Claremont Graduate School (currently known as Claremont Graduate University).

15

Knowledge Lecture IV

1989

Our topic for tonight is the knowledge-based organization. And perhaps the best way to get going is to try to visualize what a business may look like 10, 12, 15 years ahead.

It is a fairly reasonable assumption that the typical business is likely to be quite a bit larger in terms of sales 10 or 12 years from now because, barring major war or tremendous economic collapse, the economies of the developed countries are likely to grow pretty fast—and that's even without the fairly substantial boost that may come from the opening of Eastern Europe. At the same time, let me say that business will employ on its own payroll probably no more than a quarter or a third of the people it employs now.

Notice that I said "on its own payroll." I didn't say that the number of people who work for this business would decline that way.

Yes, a large part of it will be fairly steady shrinkage of blue-collar labor. I sat down the other day with the chairman of one of the world's very largest automobile companies, and its blue-collar labor is down 40 percent over the last 10 years. And we talked about that, to survive Japanese competition, it will have to cut its blue-collar labor in the next 10 years by another 40 percent. In order to get union cooperation it will have to give job security, while slashing its blue-collar payroll, which is not an easy act, if it can be done at all.

Very little of this has to do with automation, new machinery. Practically all of it comes from reorganizing the workflow, doing a more intelligent job of scheduling, of getting parts to where they are needed, when they are needed. In other words, it's simply a matter of better management rather than of investment in machinery. The organization 15 years from now will be very much flatter. GM has 28 levels of management today, and you know the old rule we laid down in the '40s that for you to really judge someone's performance, that person really has to be on the job three to five years. And if you multiply 28 by 5, you see that at GM you really have to be 140 years old before you can be considered for senior management position—and sometimes they behave like it.

For the last 20 years, I have been saying that I don't know a single large company where eliminating one level of vice presidents, no matter which, wouldn't double output. And, finally I'm being proven right. The main reason is that in the traditional organization, we did two things. First, by copying the command model of the Army, we built in an enormous amount of redundancy that you have to have on the battlefield. And, secondly, we've used management levels as information relays. And as we get to learn how to build information systems—and, believe me, we are learning very fast—a good many of these levels of management will simply prove redundant. So you will get much flatter organizations, which will also be organized far more on the basis of direct responsibility.

But the single most important reason for the decrease in the number of people who are on the company payroll is that more and more of the work is going to be farmed out. You go back 30 years, and there was not one American hospital that farmed out either its patient feeding or its housekeeping. Today, very few American hospitals do either. Most of that work is farmed out. And there are still quite a few colleges left that do their own feeding, but they are today a distinct minority; increasingly, college dormitories are not run by the colleges but by contractors. And one of the largest architectural firms in the world is just now spinning off its drafting work into a company in which the architect will own 49 percent, the draftsmen 51 percent. The architecture firm has 63 offices worldwide, which go from Sydney to Taipei to Austria. But they will do all their drafting work out of Kentucky.

Five years ago those architects could not have put their drafting work in Kentucky. But now with fax machines, there's no problem. The head office can get what it needs, and draftsmen don't have to meet customers and don't really make decisions, and so there is no need for them to be in downtown Los Angeles or in downtown Tokyo. With fax machines on either end, the drafting people in Lexington are next door to everybody.

You'll see more and more of this, and there are good reasons for it. First, contracting out gives you employment flexibility. You can get rid of a contractor and the contractor's people, where you can't get rid as easily of your own employees. The Japanese have been doing this for 30 years. Seventy-four percent of the people who work for Toyota are not on the Toyota payroll but on the payroll of contractors, of suppliers, and have been for a long time for a variety of larger historical reasons. This is what makes "lifetime employment" possible in Japan. Half of those on Toyota's payroll are men. The other half are women, and in Japan they are automatically considered temporary employees anyhow. And then, the supplier's employees are not Toyota employees and have no employment security. And so Toyota basically has lifetime employment for one-seventh of the people who work for it.

Demographic pressures will also force more contracting out of work. Increasingly there will be middle-aged or older women with half-grown children who will want to be in the labor force. And the great majority will not be senior VPs. The great majority will be clerks or clerk supervisors, and for them, a long commute into the city is simply too arduous. Wherever they can, these people look for jobs close to where they live rather than spending two hours stuck on the freeway trying to get to Los Angeles. And that alone will speed up the trend toward contracting out, because to supervise these people, to train them, will require an employer out here in the Pomona Valley [east of downtown Los Angeles] that has critical mass. And that means somebody who has multiple clients and is therefore an independent contractor.

Another thing to say is that 12 years out, even a fairly small business—and perhaps a great many nonbusinesses, too—will have to be managed in contemplation of a world economy. I'm pretty careful in my choice of words. I didn't say, "It will have to be *in* the world economy." That's very fashionable to say today, and it's silly. Most businesses, the overwhelming majority, will not be in the world economy, actively.

If you are a textile manufacturer in Denmark, you have to buy your cotton outside of Denmark. But that doesn't mean that you are in the world economy; it means that you buy a commodity. And if you buy spinning machinery, you buy it in Switzerland because that's where the best textile machinery comes from. But, again, you are not in the world economy. You sell your goods probably only in Denmark, and maybe you export a little bit just south of the border into Northern Germany. But that's it. Your market is pretty local, within 100 kilometers, two hours by car, and that's very typical. And that's not going to change that much. And yet that Danish cotton textile manufacturer not only reads the cotton market commodity prices every day very carefully but he also pays attention to what goes on in the textile industry all over the world—or he won't last long. He has to manage in contemplation of the world economy even though his market is pretty much a local one and probably doesn't go beyond the Danish language area much. The assumption is not that every place is your market but, rather, that every place is your competitor.

Another thing that you will see increasingly over the next 12 years is partnerships. And so you will have to learn to work with people who are not your employees but who are also not outsiders—you know, like the nice North Carolina phrase "kissing kin." And this is going to be a very great challenge. It means, above all, that you have to be much clearer in your objectives, your policies, and your strategy because you can't just change rapidly. You can't order people and say, "You'll do this or else you'll walk the plank." And this means that five years before you do something you'll have to think it through, because it will take you that long to persuade people.

Most of us still think that when we talk of personnel relations, we talk of rank and file. That's not going to be where the problems are. When you eliminate levels of management, you demote managers. You may pay them more; you may give them wonderful titles such as "senior associate." But nobody is fooled by that. And the less power people have, the more they lay claim to it. And so the resistance will be incredible. Those MBAs come in with the wrong expectations today. They expect to be managers, but they aren't going to be. They are going to be specialists—very well paid, but not managers, because there aren't going to be that many management positions. And so they will feel betrayed, and it's already beginning.

The American automobile industry has tried very hard in the last few years to bring in cooperation with the union rank and file, and everybody expected tremendous resistance on the plant floor. In fact, there has been virtually none. Instead, the resistance has come from the supervisors and from the union general stewards. Suddenly, the personnel people in the automobile companies must concentrate not on the rank and file but on the union management people and their own foremen. You will see more and more of this, and it and will strengthen the personnel function, for better or worse.

And finally, in 10 or 15 years we will have been forced to tackle the basic problem of the legitimacy and accountability of management. Whenever the organization of production changes—and I am stepping on a minefield here—new social classes emerge as the dominant groups. A little over a thousand years ago, the machine first became a tool of production in the West. Before 800, the windmill and the waterwheel were toys. But then they became tools of production in the Europe of 1800. A little later, the spinning wheel came in, invented probably in China but really used primarily in Europe.

And out of the Middle East, out of Persia, came the stirrup and the horse collar. And the new class that emerged as dominant was the feudal knight. Suddenly you could fight on horseback because you had the stirrup, and you had the horse collar. Before that, you couldn't shoot off an arrow without being thrown backward. You couldn't do it because you had to put your feet on the ground, and the stirrup gave you that place. Otherwise, Newton's Second Law—you know, "to every action there is a reaction"—would just have thrown you over the horse. And so the feudal knight became one dominant group. The other one was the craftsman. The city of antiquity was not the city of craftsmen; it was the city of slaves, primarily. And suddenly you had the craftsmen and the craftsmen's guild and the Swiss weavers and the shoemakers and the armorers and the goldsmiths and the wheelwrights, and they dominated the new phenomenon—the city, the occident or the Western city. And 800 years later, at the end of the seventeenth century, the steam engine was designed. And while the old classes didn't disappear, they became marginal. The new dominant ones were the blue-collar industry worker and what we usually mean when we say capitalists—that is, people who knew how to use money to organize production.

And now, with information becoming the new principle of organization, what are the new classes? The blue-collar worker is already pretty much gone as a determining class. I'm not saying just in numbers, but they are no longer center stage. They may still get an Oscar for best supporting role, but nobody buys a ticket to see the best supporting role. The knowledge worker is rapidly taking center stage.

Who is going to succeed the capitalist? Well, it is pretty clear who it is because that person is already on stage: it is the manager. But then, to whom and for what is management accountable? The capitalist says only to the stockholders. We know that that's not good enough. It is predictable that those economies that are going to grow and develop will not be dominated by immediate stockholders' gains, because that's too short run, and most of the things you have to do to create wealth-producing capacity take five to ten years.

So let me say we will need much less money. When you look at the new industries—software compared with an integrated steel mill—they are not capital intensive. This is not to say that money will be unimportant. But it will mean that you can't base control on the ability to marshal capital for productivity. Instead, it will be based on an ability to marshal the scarce critical resource of knowledge.

This then raises questions: What is performance? How is it measured? How do you prevent abuse of power—and a lot of what you have seen in the conglomerates is abuse of power because the only purpose of the conglomeration was to enrich management and to feed its vanity. It served no economic purpose, and that's abuse of power. What is the balance between short range and long range, the balance between market standing and profitability, the balance between innovation and continuity?

All of these things, which we can talk about learnedly but can't really define or measure, will be up for grabs. And we will have a replay of an issue that agitated the early years of this century—the polarity between what Thorstein Veblen, the great sociologist of that period, called the instinct of workmanship and the acquisitive instinct. In other words, they are both performance, but they are very different kinds of performance. And you need both. You need economic performance and you need the instinct of workmanship, which if you use present-day terms you would call marketing and innovation.

So when it comes to the information-based organization 10 years hence, one can already delineate some major challenges—the challenge of converting middle management into expert professionals, professional contributors rather than people whose work it is to make others productive. Now, they must make themselves productive.

From a lecture delivered at Claremont Graduate School (currently known as Claremont Graduate University).

16

Knowledge Lecture V

1989

Good evening, Ladies and Gentlemen, and welcome to our last session. And before—in case I forget—let me wish you all a very, very Merry Christmas and a very happy New Year.

As you know, our last topic is *you*. So far, we have been up in assorted stratospheres talking about major changes in society, major changes in organization, and today we are going to discuss what all this means for the people who not only do the work but also have to live in this kind of world and society and organization and have to achieve and make their careers and make their contribution. And perhaps I'll start with something that may kind of surprise you. Let me say that whenever during the last, oh, 35 years anybody has asked me, "What is the best management book?" I found it very easy to answer. I've always said, "It's Alfred Sloan's *My Years with General Motors*." I still say that, and the book came out in 1964 when Sloan was 88, 89. And I have gone back and referred to it and looked into it and read up in it, but I have not really, for 35 years, read it very carefully until a few weeks ago. Sloan's publisher, Doubleday, came to me and said, "We are planning a new issue of that book, and would you be willing to write the preface for it?" And in a weak moment, I said, "Yes."

And so, I had to reread the book, and I was tremendously impressed. It is probably the best book of case studies in business management there is. Each chapter is a case study. And the thing that hit me was that even though a good many of these cases took place in the 1920s or '30s, and basically the book comes to an end with World War II, really nothing new has happened. These are exactly the kind of situations that you will encounter and your successors will encounter in your companies. And it reminded me of a very wise man I knew. This must have been around 1960 when we talked about the tremendous explosion and expansion of management. And this friend of mine said, "You know, Peter, 99 percent of all managers today do exactly what managers did in 1900. There are only so many more of them." And I think this is profound wisdom.

Most of us do exactly what our ancestors did, only so many more of us are required. And that's why we now have business schools. A hundred years ago, we required a very small number of naturals who came up in the school of hard knocks. And the trouble with the school of hard knocks is that the knocks are so hard, the casualty rates are very great, and we can't afford to lose that many. That's why we have schools, which are basically a protection, a protective device.

So much of it is continuity and not novelty. To be sure, when you read that Sloan book, the terminology is occasionally a little old-fashioned. I kind of smiled because he had such a terrible time trying to describe cash flow. The word didn't exist, and he had to explain it to somebody. But it's very clear what he means. And the tools Sloan had—while he was trained as an engineer, I'm not sure he had a slide rule because he graduated before 1900. Certainly he had no computer. But the situations are exactly what you encounter today: capital appropriations, decisions in organization, decisions on how one squares the need to organize according to logic with the need to staff according to personality. That's nothing new. So let me start out by saying that, yes, the tools change, the terminology changes, the emphasis changes. But the tasks are very much the same.

The other day I sat down with a very brilliant medical scientist who is on the advanced frontier of medicine, and we talked about the tremendous quantum leap in instrumentation. And he said, "But you'll note that when it comes to what's truly essential, which is to how one looks at the patient, none of us has as good or as careful an eye as Hippocrates. And, that was 3,000 years ago, and if we could only teach that to the young doctors, the rest would be easy."

The executive of tomorrow better learn the craft, the foundations. And I say that bluntly because, people, I'm not very happy. I see a good deal of the likes of you in our executive management program, and you are weak in the fundamentals. And you are weak for two reasons. One is because you are so specialized. In this country, most people come up in a specialty until they are pretty higher up, and they don't really get the exposure to any other part of business or management in the formative years. And maybe that's a strength, but one will always pay the price. When I look at the people who are in my executive management group who are top-flight marketing people, it is amazing what they don't know about—call it quantitative, call it accounting, call it analysis. And what they don't know about managing people is a little frightening, and that's why they come to us. And I hope that's what we help them to overcome, to add the understanding of the other dimensions of a business or an organization.

Yes, one needs the latest techniques, but one needs the fundamentals. And that's addressed not only to you. That's addressed to me and to others in academia because we also forget the fundamentals. It's very easy to do. All of us tend to be specialists, and we make our careers, oh, by publishing learned research papers in a learned journal on the newest wrinkle. And we don't ourselves stress the fundamentals. We take them for granted, which is always a mistake. We need to remind ourselves—and also remind you—that no matter how advanced that physician is going to be when he practices neurosurgery, he begins by learning gross anatomy. And there has been very little that's new in gross anatomy since about 1680, very little. The bones haven't changed. We haven't added a single bone or lost one. Sure, we know a good deal more about things that baffled the great anatomists of the seventeenth century—glands and organ functions and lots of things. But fundamentally, the skeleton that you can see in Dutch paintings of the 1680s hanging in the doctor's office is the same skeleton from which a young medical student still learns gross anatomy. Those are the foundations, and if he didn't know his gross anatomy, he'd do untold damage as a neurosurgeon.

The foundations become doubly important in period of change. This is partly because one is apt to forget the fundamentals during such times, and partly because one is then prone to reinvent the wheel unless there is solid foundation. And yet there are periods in any discipline, in any practice, when you have genuine changes that are more than just refinements—that are more than just slight variations on a familiar theme.

When you look at our field, at management, we are all probably pretty far advanced in such a period of considerable change. It isn't the first one. Within the last 100 years we have had at least two—and in each of them, people have had to relearn and redirect themselves. If you go back a little over a hundred years, the contemporaries were totally baffled by the emergence of what we today call the modern business (and, incidentally, just as baffled by the emergence of the modern university and the emergence of the modern civil service). They couldn't figure it out. It just didn't fit with anything anybody knew.

To a large extent this was a gross misunderstanding of the emergence of people who for the first time combined what had until then been totally separate functions. One was the merchant function. Another was the capitalist function. And another was the inventor function or the entrepreneur function.

These had been separate and discreet, and suddenly you had people emerge—whether it was a J.P. Morgan or an Andrew Carnegie or a John D. Rockefeller or the people who built Singer sewing machine or International Harvest or General Electric or the telephone company—very different people who somehow seemed to combine things that didn't belong together, at least not in the way people had always looked at them. Accept the fact that those who do new things are always suspected of sorcery and of black magic, and yet when you look back in retrospect, they were groping for building what we today call organizations capable of continuity.

And then, as you know, after World War II we had another period of change. Up to that time, while quite a few people worked in organizations, very few of them were conscious of the phenomenon. Suddenly, we saw it. And you got into an age that the literature of the '50s and '60s described as being of *The Organization Man* [William Whyte's 1956 sociological commentary] and *The Man in the Gray Flannel Suit* [Sloan Wilson's 1955 novel]. And the people who worked and lived in large organizations seemed to be totally impermeable to change. And, believe me, this is what stimulated the enormous explosion of the business school. And this is one reason why the business school in the next 20 years will have to change a great deal. We have well-trained but also very narrow people who together are a very, very strong army but individually make a very minor contribution. When you look back at the literature today, it was a gross exaggeration and caricature, but it captured some things that existed or at least a tendency that existed. And that was a great change in the perception of people and their vision. In a way it started in this country, but it pervaded the whole world—and no place more than Japan.

Now we may be halfway, or a quarter of the way, into another change: Information is becoming the organizing principle of organizations. And what does this mean for the individual?

Let me say again that it means that you'd better know the fundamentals. It is dangerous to acquire advanced new techniques without knowing the fundamentals. It is dangerous because it is self-defeating. You don't understand the basic assumptions; you don't understand the limitations. And so you are a virtuoso, but you don't make music. You make noise very fast, and that isn't the same thing as making music.

From a lecture delivered at Claremont Graduate School (currently known as Claremont Graduate University).

PART VI

1990s

In 1990, Peter Drucker published the book *Managing the Nonprofit Organization: Principles and Practices*. Although best known for advising top executives from Sears, General Electric, Citicorp, and other major corporations, Drucker also counseled numerous social-sector organizations such as the Girl Scouts, Salvation Army, and CARE. His advice was wide ranging but, more than anything, he forced these organizations (and many, many others) to tackle five fundamental questions that every enterprise—profit or nonprofit—should be required to answer: *What is our mission? Who is our customer? What does the customer value? What are our results? What is our plan?* Drucker had worked closely with nonprofits beginning in the 1940s. But his interest intensified over time as he came to view the social sector as the sphere that "gives purpose, gives direction." Originally, Drucker had hoped that individuals would find these qualities in their day jobs, through what he called the "plant community." But, as more and more factories closed and job security grew ever more elusive, he conceded that "the plant community never took root." This, in turn, made nonprofits all the more crucial—not only for the recipients of their services but for their volunteers as well. "Citizenship in and through the social sector is not a panacea" for the problems that we face, Drucker wrote in his 1993 book *Post-Capitalist Society*. "But it may be a prerequisite for tackling these ills. It restores the civic responsibility that is the mark of citizenship, and the civic pride that is the mark of community."

17

The New Priorities

1991

I'm an old historian and one of the things that are mysteries to historians is those periods every 200 or 300 years when suddenly the world changes. It's like turning a kaleidoscope—the pieces are the same, but their meaning is totally different. And the people who survived that period usually can't even figure out what the world was like before it changed. That was the situation around 1500. Next door to us is the wonderful exhibition of the World of Columbus in 1492. That was such a period of change. We have a letter from a very distinguished man of 1525 after the Reformation who said, "I've been trying to explain to my son what the world looked like when I grew up in the 1480s, and I can't." And we had the same phenomenon 200 years ago. It began with the American Revolution, and 50 years later, after the Napoleonic Wars, I don't think anybody could have understood what the world was like when his father was born.

We are living in such a period. My guess is that we're more than halfway through. But only about halfway. It's a period that began around 1973, and it's been moving very fast. Just to show you how fast, I published a book [*The New Realities*] that I finished around September 1988. I published it in the spring of '89. And it predicted—it didn't predict, it just took notice of the impending collapse of Communism and the dissolution of the Communist empire. It came out in early '89, two-and-a-half years ago, and every reviewer said, "This man is crazy." And my publisher asked Henry Kissinger to review it, and Henry wrote back and said, "I have known Peter for many years. I don't want to say that he has become gaga." That was early 1989. For the first time in my 40 years with that publisher, he made me take out the sentence in which I said that I consider it highly probable that within the next five years, Germany will be reunified. He said, "Look, Peter, at your age, you don't have to make a total ass of yourself."

And I didn't predict; I just looked out the window. I don't predict. I learned that in 1929. I got my first decent job with a major English newspaper, and I predicted in October '29 that the New York Stock Exchange crash couldn't last. I'm not going to predict anymore. So, no, I just looked out the window. And that's only two-and-a-half years ago. It was very clear that Mr. Gorbachev couldn't succeed. You didn't have to predict it. It was very clear that the Russian empire would dissolve. You didn't have to predict it. But nobody could imagine it.

As you know, Mr. James Baker, the secretary of state, slipped into one of his speeches a very innocent-sounding sentence in which he basically said, "We, in the United States, are now ready for the dissolution of China." He didn't put it this way. He put it very diplomatically, but everybody got the message. And I think it very likely that by the end of the century we will be back to the traditional China, which has a nominal central government that costs a lot of money—and that's about all it does—and where you have economic warlords overseeing different regions. China will also be the center of an economic Far Eastern union.

And so, we are in a period of very rapid change, and some of the elements of the new worldview are already pretty clear. Maybe the most important thing is that, since about the French Revolution, we in the developed countries have believed in salvation by society, the secular religion of which Communism was the most extreme manifestation. One of my first good jobs was as the *Manchester Guardian's* correspondent in Moscow in 1929, which by the way cured me of ever becoming a left-winger. That was the year Stalin liquidated 20 million *kulaks*, and I still wake up at night with the screaming jeebees and nightmares. But that was only the extreme manifestation of a worldwide belief that by changing society, you could change the old Adam and create the new Adam, the perfect man. And that belief is gone. It peaked in this country in the Kennedy years. And now it's gone. The belief in salvation by society is gone.

Whether we are going to come back to an age in which faith again becomes important, or whether we are entering an age in which there is no such thing as any kind of belief, I don't know. But we no longer believe in salvation by society. There is no way of restoring it.

Another thing is exceedingly important. For 200 years, the question was: What *should* government do? In 1792, a very bright cookie asked the question: What *can* government do? Nobody listened. For 200 years, the only question was what government *should* do, not what it *can* do. As recently as 1944, a very eminent social philosopher and economist [Friedrich von Hayek] published a book called *The Road to Serfdom*. The author only said that if government does it, this means tyranny. Nobody doubted what government could do. The only difference was between countries like ours, in which we said government had better be limited not for the sake of efficiency but for the sake of freedom, and countries that put efficiency first. And that also peaked, I would say, around the late 1960s. But now, "What *can* government do?" is again the question.

In 1968, I published a book [*The Age of Discontinuity*] in which I coined the word *privatization*. Government would never privatize, yet it was very clear that we had reached the end of the question of what government should do. The question "what *can* government do?" is not easy, by the way. I came to this country and this town in 1937 as a correspondent for a group of British papers, and coming out of Europe it was an incredible revelation to see practically every one of the New Deal programs work. Some of them were perhaps not well conceived, but they worked. And not one government program since 1950 has worked.

And not only in this country. The only exception is Japan, and there it's beginning not to work now. But otherwise, whether you look at Britain or Germany or France, there isn't a single government program that has worked. They all have the same results of costing a hell of a lot of money and usually creating a beautiful neoclassical building and that's it. There is not a person in this room or in this country who believes that if Congress or the president announces a new program, it will work. You're all total cynics, which is dangerous, by the way. All we say is, "well, how much is it going to cost?" But nobody asks, "what is it going to do?" because nobody believes in it anymore. And that is not cynicism; that's experience. Ask the question, simply: "What can government do?" It's a question that hasn't been asked for 200 years. What is the competence of government? Not: what are the good intentions of government?

Another thing you can see is that we're moving into an economy for which there was no precedent until the European Economic Community triggered it. But whether you like it or not—and not all of us like it—we have a North American economic community. It's almost irrelevant whether Congress passes the customs union or not, because integration is 80 percent complete.

Fifty years hence, I think it's predictable that historians will say that what is happening in North America is more important than what's happened in Europe. If you had told anybody 10 years ago that a Mexican government would ask for a customs union with the United States, everybody would have given you a horse laugh. I don't know how well you know Mexico, but Mexican history can be summed up in one sentence: The objective of Mexico was to make the Rio Grande a little wider than the Atlantic Ocean. A Mexican proverb says, "If you are in bed with an elephant, it doesn't help you that the elephant means well." And this elephant hasn't always meant well, by the way. And yet Mexican policies—all of which had one goal to make Mexico economically and culturally independent of those nasty, pushy, aggressive, dangerous Yankees—has been a total failure. And so they finally accepted that if you can't lick them you have to join them. That's one of the greatest reversals in history.

It is now 500 years since Columbus thought he had found Japan and instead found America, and we are now in the process of rediscovering America. For 500 years, all relationships in the New World were not with the New World but with the Old World. My wife has Argentinean cousins who went to Argentina in 1852 and every one of them went to school back to England until the current generation. Her cousin, Roberto, went to the Massachusetts Institute of Technology. And only now, we in this country still don't know Latin America, but Latin America now looks north instead of looking east. And we are beginning to be very skeptical about all those predictions about the Pacific Rim. I think the real integration is going to be within the Americas.

We've also moved from a society in which capital was its scarce resource into one in which knowledge is the scarce resource. If you have the knowledge, you can get the money. The Japanese government now pays you to move factories out of Japan, not because there is a scarcity of blue-collar labor there, but because blue-collar labor offers a very poor return on society's investment. By the time a kid has finished high school—whether having learned anything or not is another matter—you have an investment close to a hundred thousand bucks, and you don't get it back if that youngster becomes a blue-collar worker. You have to make sure that he or she in Japan becomes a knowledge worker. The Japanese haven't pronounced it openly because it is very unpopular, but they have reached the point where they consider blue-collar labor a liability, not an asset. We still think it's a factor in production. The Japanese consider it a drag on production. As a Japanese friend, one of my ex-students who is now a vice minister, said: "Look at the demographics of the world for the next 40 years. There is going to be no shortage of people in Latin America, in East Asia. There is going to be no shortage of people for manufacturing. Far from it. To worry about it as you Americans do is just plain silly."

So, what are some of the priorities out of this? First, let me say a word about what we call mistakenly the nonprofit sector. That's a legal term, a tax-collector term. I call it a higher profit sector. Nine hundred thousand nonprofit organizations exist in this country, plus or minus. Thirty thousand new ones are created each year. That is a uniquely American phenomenon. By the year 2000, they will have doubled their share of the gross national product, which is about 3 percent. Nonprofits get three to four times the effectiveness out of their resources. The government, no matter who gets elected, will retrench. The deficit cannot be maintained. And if we don't want to have serious social problems, we have to increase the effectiveness and the resources of the nonprofit sector. That's almost priority number one over the next few years, or we'll be in very serious trouble.

Priority number two: A little over a century ago, we began to work on the productivity of people who make and move things. That has been the great explosion, increasing 50-fold in 110 years. It's totally unprecedented. Most of those gains were not taken in the form of material goods. More than 50 percent of the productivity gains have been taken in the form of less work. Don't call it leisure, necessarily. In 1909, the year I was born, almost everybody in the developed world worked 3,300 hours a year, except a very few rich people. Today, the Japanese still work more than anybody else—2,000 hours a year. We in this country work 1,800 hours a year, the Germans, 1,650. Now, you may say not all of it has been well spent; five hours a day watching television may be a very poor use of extra hours. But that's the way it is.

Today, this no longer counts because less than one-fifth of the labor force in developing countries makes and moves things. Eighty percent are in knowledge work and service work, where the productivity is miserable, to put it mildly. In fact, there ain't none. Does anybody here believe that the teacher of 1991 is more productive than the teacher of 1900? And service work is worse. The productivity of knowledge work and the dignity of service work are our next big priority, and there's not a blessed thing that government can do to help. This is what employers have to work on.

The third priority, and it's going to be a difficult one, is that we are shifting from a world in which bigness matters to a world in which bigness is irrelevant. You know, the elephant is not a more effective animal than the cockroach. In fact, cockroaches— as all of you in Washington know—will survive all of us. No, size is functional, and the advantages of bigness are gone with information. And so we have a very real question: How do we make this transition to a world in which yesterday's bigness no longer helps and is actually in many cases a severe disadvantage? We are moving into structural change where size follows function and by itself confers no advantage. Size becomes a strategic choice, and I think one of the priorities for business is to think through what the right size is for us, where we really fit our logical niche.

So we face a very different world with very different priorities. And as I said, we are halfway through this period, or a little more. By the year 2015 we will be over it, but the next 25 years will still be years of very fast, unprecedented change. We can just begin to see, very dimly, the outline of that new structure.

Governments will have to think through what they can do, but at the same time increasingly they are going to be transnational. The environment can only be dealt with transnationally. Last year, for the first time in history—my degree is in international law—all countries banded together, regardless of their interests, to put down terrorism. That's one of the great turning points in history. I think you will see the same thing happening with respect to North Korea. That's a transnational task. So we have transnational tasks, national tasks, and local tasks. That's a very different world from that of political scientists who saw the national government as the only power center and center of action. And you can see that already pretty clearly. We just don't quite know how to organize it.

From a speech given at the Economic Club of Washington.

18

Do You Know Where You Belong?

1992

When I look at people who have done a good job in managing their career—and I don't just mean in terms of jobs and money and title, but in terms of achievement and satisfaction and contribution—these are people who build a network. This is a modern term. We didn't speak of it 10 years ago. Back then, we said, "These are people who keep in touch." Today, they build a network.

In a way, they have learned how to be considerate. And, believe me, I don't think people are born considerate. There are some people who are born more polite than others. But considerate? No. Considerate is doing a few elementary things.

The first is to have a tickler file in which you have enough information about the people you work with to be considerate. To call up and say, "Mary this is your wedding anniversary—20 years. Isn't it wonderful? Congratulations." And you know, those of us who have been married a long time have learned that the husband had better not forget the wedding anniversary. But no husband remembers it after 35 years, so we have it in our calendar. We have a tickler file. And one learns that you keep a tickler file with the names of the children of the people you work with, and their birthdays, and their wedding anniversaries. And that's being considerate. That's showing respect.

You also don't lose touch with the people with whom you've worked. And it's not just sending a Christmas card. And, by the way, don't send that canned Christmas card—the Xeroxed one that begins, "It's been a very eventful year for the Jonas family. Our grandchild got his first tooth . . ." Don't send that one.

But when you're in Tacoma, pick up the telephone and call that fellow who has been transferred there and say, "Joe, I'm in town. I don't know whether I have enough time to get together with you. But I just wanted to say hello and find out how you're doing." Keep the network.

In the first place, you may need it. During the last three years, an enormous number of people have been forced to find another job. Maybe you've been with the same big company for 26 years. You've never had to write your résumé. One more promotion and suddenly, at age 49, you're out. It's traumatic and painful.

And we've had study after study on what makes the difference between those who were able to find a new job relatively easy and those who couldn't. What kind of experience and expertise you have makes a lot of difference. But when it comes to people of the same age, with the same expertise and the same background, the ones who do well are the ones who know where they belong. They know their strengths, know their performance, and can position themselves. The other difference for those who do well is that they have a network. They've never lost touch.

These are not close friends, but they are people who know you and whom you know. And again and again, when one of them gets that letter or telephone call, he calls right back and says, "Gregory, I think have a job that might interest you. Do you mind if I talk to my friend Joe down the street about it?" And two weeks later you have an interview with Joe.

Again and again, this is a balance between how you present yourself—not bragging about yourself but knowing yourself. And knowing how to maneuver yourself, which is what a network really is. It isn't being popular. It is being considerate, and not using people just as tools but as people.

Another skill: Make sure that before you are in your forties you have a real outside activity. Not just a hobby but an activity. First, it creates an entirely different network. I teach a fairly large executive management class—about 60 people. A number of them are from the aerospace industry, which has been very turbulent for three years now. And at least half of them have had to change jobs. And so I said, "How did you get that new job?" You'd be surprised how many of them say, "Marianne and I belong to that church and we are volunteers together. And when that big aircraft company laid me off, it was through the other volunteers in that church that I immediately found leads." It's another network. And it is one very powerful one, by the way.

But that is the lesser importance. Its major importance is what it does to keep you alive and to enrich you. Believe me, very few jobs still have challenges after 20 years. The worst are those brilliant young college professors who begin to teach French history at age 28 and love it and are excited and bubble over, and every day is sheer joy. And 50 years later, they're bored even by their own jokes. And so is the class. And that's when people say they're burned out. No, they're not. They're bored. They need another challenge.

There are two kinds of challenges. The more important—and the easier—one is what I have come to call the parallel career. In this country, half of our adults work as a volunteer for at least three hours in a nonprofit agency of some sort. And for many, this is no longer addressing envelopes. They run their church. They run the training program for the Girl Scout Council. They design the training program. This is an unpaid management job, an executive job. In some cases, it offers more responsibility than what they have at the bank or the insurance company or in the trucking company. And it keeps them alive. It's a new challenge.

It's a new environment. It's different people. And if forces you to remain adaptively innovative.

When I look at those college professors at age 43, I realize that a good many of them should now do something else. They are not going to produce those great scholarly books they talked about 15 years ago. There were those two little magazine articles, that's all. They are no longer the greatest classroom teachers, if they ever were. They have lost all flexibility, all elasticity. They are stuck. Not in the routine. It shouldn't be a routine. They are stuck in their own kind of premature aging. And then I look at the ones who are different. And almost without expectation, here is that colleague at age 46 who is not a very great scholar but he is still full of enthusiasm in his classroom. He runs one of the Boy Scout troops on the side. And every weekend is a new challenge. Nine-year-old boys are a new challenge every weekend. He comes back from that weekend totally exhausted and just full of ideas.

Keep that in mind. You need that outside activity precisely because the job tends to become all embracing, precisely because you take work home at night. But it's also because the great majority of us reach the ceiling in terms of advancement and promotion in our early forties.

You need something that is not routine, and you need to build it into your life early—something that is meaningful to you, that cause you believe in. Something where you can contribute, where you can take leadership. Something where you can say, "I'm making a contribution."

At the same time, you should also learn to look at yourself and assess, "When do I belong elsewhere? When do I not need a parallel career but a second career?"

Go back not very long—make it a hundred years. At age 43, that farmer in North Dakota was a very old man, and his wife was a very old woman, if she was still alive. And he was no longer capable of working. If he hadn't been injured—and most of them were—the work was terribly hard. And there were those lonely winters with the howling wind, day in and day out. It took a heavy toll. Now, that farmer in the North Dakota prairie didn't expect fulfillment from his job. All he hoped was that he would be able to feed his children over the winter, and it was touch and go. It was a living. It wasn't a life. And the steelworker didn't expect fulfillment out of the job. He expected paychecks that would enable him to feed his children.

But knowledge workers expect fulfillment. We also don't get injured anymore. Sitting behind a desk, the worst work-related injury we can expect is hemorrhoids. And that doesn't disable you. And so now we have very long working lives. And we will have to learn to take responsibility not just for a parallel career but also for a second career. How do I repot myself? At what age?

And when the job becomes simply a place to hang your hat, when it's "Thank God It's Friday," when you begin to play games with yourself so that it makes the job more complicated, then you are bored. And boredom is a deadly disease. You need to be challenged. The great danger is that you live physically long and die mentally too soon, and the waste I see of ability and talent is dreadful. So don't say, "I'm stuck in the groove." Say, "Where do I belong? What do I have to contribute?"

From part of a lecture series for George Washington University.

19

The Era of the Social Sector

———

1994

Let me start out by saying that it is a great pleasure to be here today and to talk about the nonprofit organization: why we need it, what it will have to do, and what its requirements and problems are.

Manufacturing today is going the way of farming. New jobs are there and plentiful; they are good jobs largely, but different jobs. They require, above all, a great deal of formal education and a great deal of skill, and so they are not jobs in which people out of the factory can easily move into the way farmers 30 years ago could easily move off a very poor farm into well-paid factory jobs with high job security.

This is a social transition. It is not something in which government can do very much. In fact, the problems we now face are not problems government is good at dealing with. Governments are very good at doing things that embrace the entire nation, but most of the tasks we have today are local and are not done well by a central bureaucracy. They are done well on the local level. Most of them are very specific jobs. They require organizations and institutions that are very, very narrowly focused.

Let me give just a few examples, and I think that they would apply to Japan just as much as they apply to any other developed country. We need to retrain workers, and that is a crying need that we know cannot be fulfilled except very locally, working with the people who are going to employ the workers of tomorrow. We know a great deal about training people. These are people with very limited horizons, and limited experiences, and limited time spans. So the need is to have people retrained where the next job is, and for the next job. This is not something that you can do by having an educational program. But we also have tremendous educational needs for the educated people. Technology is changing so fast and not just in high tech; it's changing even faster in medicine. I have a nephew who is a prominent radiologist; he is probably the best-known professor of radiology in the United States. He said to me, "You know, Uncle Peter, if I do not go back to school every three years for a six-week course, I am obsolete."

We need it for teachers, especially in the university where, bluntly, the level of teaching today is very, very poor all over the world. We need it for almost every profession—for accountants and for managers. We need to have facilities for the continuing education of already highly educated adults. This, again, is a local need. It's undertaken by this university and by that university.

We also need nonprofits to meet local social needs. Take the rehabilitation of alcoholics, which we now know how to do. Thirty years ago we did not. Today we know how to do it with a fairly high success rate. We can rehabilitate 50 percent, maybe 60 percent. But it's done locally. And it is done by local groups, made up mostly of ex-alcoholics, but it is not done nationally. All government programs to rehabilitate alcoholics or drug addicts have failed. Local volunteer programs staffed by volunteers— and mostly by people who have been in that predicament themselves—are remarkably successful.

We need local volunteers, as well, for what is one of our greatest needs: to organize the systematic exposure of young people to foreign cultures. You know, three of my four children, when they were young, worked abroad. One in Japan for three years, one in France, and one in South America. And it made an incredible difference to them; it changed their basic outlook. Now two of my grandsons have lived in Japan. As young people, one studied here in high school for the better part of a year, and the other, after he had finished college, worked in Japan as a software designer for six months. This made an enormous difference to them. We've been able to do this because we have friends all over the world, but this is not the right way to do it. It needs organization. It needs to be done professionally, rather than haphazardly. And that requires another nonprofit institution, and so it goes on and on and on. While government can encourage these things, it cannot do them. They have to be done locally. And they have to be done in large measure by volunteers.

There is another need. When I grew up, most people lived in a very narrow community and could not escape the small village, such as the valley in which my ancestors lived for several hundred years in England. Community was fate. You were born into it and you could not get out. Now that is gone. Most of our young people today live in big cities. They live a much better life than their ancestors did in material terms. They are educated. Yet they have no community.

We need citizenship; all we can do in our modern democracies is vote and pay taxes. That is not enough to be citizens. To be citizens, you have to be able to do something where you see results. And so the tremendous growth of the volunteer in the West began in the United States, where we have the oldest tradition, and this movement is now rapidly coming up in Western Europe. This answers a need of today's people—a need for something where they can first choose what they are doing. One chooses to work in international education, and then the next one in rehabilitation of criminals or of alcoholics, and the third one in teaching disabled children. These are choices, and they are meaningful to people.

My youngest daughter, who is a very successful banker and married and has two children, is the financial officer—unpaid, of course—of the school district in which she lives. It has about 15,000 students. And though she spends two evenings a week on that, she considers it her real contribution. She finds her job at the bank, where she is very well paid, to be very interesting. But she doesn't feel that she is contributing something that corresponds to her values.

The commitment when I first came to Japan [in 1959] of the entire country to rebuild was overwhelming. Japan had been badly hurt, not just hurt physically, but even more hurt morally. Its pride was hurt. That enormous need to rebuild, that commitment, was overwhelming.

I went back home to the United States and told everybody that Japan would be the next major economic power. In the '50s, everybody thought I was crazy. Statistics didn't prove it; but the spirit was there—the commitment that "I make a difference." Now that has been achieved. People like their jobs and are well paid, and they like their companies. But there is no longer the commitment that "I make a difference." And without it, a nation very soon begins to fall apart. It loses its heart, its soul. We need a sector in which an individual can make a difference, can make a commitment. We need the nonprofit sector.

Let me say that this is not something that should come as a great surprise to you in Japan because, though I am afraid most of you do not know it, you have probably the richest tradition of community organization and community service and community responsibility of any major country in the world. Sixty years ago, when I was a very young economist working in a bank in London, I began by pure accident to get interested in Japanese art and then in Japanese history. One of the things that was amazing to me was the tremendous community culture of the Edo period [1603 to 1868]. This was reflected by the extent to which that village or that *han* [local fief] took responsibility for the local needs.

Long before there was compulsory education in Japan, the country was almost completely literate—the first nation in the world to have universal literacy. That was the result of a hundred years of volunteer-based, nonprofit institutions in which in every *han*, the *bunjin* [the literati] started schools. Most of them were poorly supported by the *daimyo* [feudal lords], but largely supported by the community, some for *samurai* [the warrior class] only, many more for anybody who was willing to work hard. I don't know whether you know, but every single one of the men who built Meiji [the period from 1868 to 1912 in which Japan rose to be a world power] came out of one of those *bunjin* schools—volunteer, nonprofit, local organizations.

So you have an enormously rich tradition. Next to the United States, where we have an enormous tradition of community service built around the church, you in Japan may have the richest tradition of community organization, of community association, of nonprofit organizations. Now is the time to rediscover it and put it to work again because government cannot do it. In the next 20 or 30 years, governments are not going to become stronger unless they become dictatorships. They will become weaker. They have taken on too many things. They have outgrown their financial resources. You in Japan are the only country that is not bankrupt. Every other government in the developed world is bankrupt and cannot raise taxes. If they do, it will only create inflation or recession. They have to retrench, and they cannot take on new tasks. Besides, these are not tasks that government is good at. These are tasks that have to be done in the local community.

We are talking of something that is neither government nor business. We in the United States and the West began about 60 or 70 years ago to talk of the two sectors: the "private sector," which is business, and the "public sector" that is government.

What we are going to build in the next 30 or 40 years is the third sector—the "social sector." Government will be in it; government has a part to play. And business will be very heavily in it. This is perhaps more so in Japan than any other country simply because your businesses are so much more organized. With the big *keiretsu* [networks of companies forged through historical association and cross-ownership], with the main banks, and with organized industry groups, business can act. So I think, yes, in Japan the social sector will depend very heavily on business—not just on business money but on business leadership, on business participation.

The signs are there. When I look at Japan, there is nothing in the world that can compare to the *Keidanren* [the Federation of Economic Organizations]. Not just in power, but in responsibility. Sure, it represents an interest group, big business mostly, but it represents big business in society. There is nothing like that in any other country. So, you already have a very strong social nonprofit sector. You are not aware of it, perhaps.

This is going to be—and I think one can confidently predict it—the growth area of a modern developed society. It is going to be incredibly diverse, because the needs are so diverse, because society today is so diverse. There is the need to maintain a neighborhood and to keep the environment from being polluted, and the need to do something about learning-disabled children. And then you have rehabilitation needs; there are so many old people who survive way beyond any earlier time span but need help. Maybe they have had a knee replaced, and they need somebody to work with them on learning to walk again. Or maybe they have had a stroke, and they need to work with somebody to learn to speak again. These are volunteer needs. Sure you must have a professional to lead and supervise, but the work is very largely by people who say, "This is my neighbor; these are the people in my community."

And so we have all kinds of social needs. But we also know one thing: A nonprofit agency has to be specialized. It does one thing. Yesterday, I had lunch with a group of friends of our host here today and it was very interesting. There was a gentleman there who represented motorboat fans, a kind of sporting club. Next to him was somebody from an environmental group; and the motorboat man is not a bit concerned about the environment, and the environment man is not a bit concerned about motorboats. That way they are effective. They have a single purpose with a single focus, something to believe in, something they are committed to; and that is what a nonprofit requires.

Most people here who know me think of me as somebody concerned with business management, and so do most people in the United States. But that is a misunderstanding. I learned almost 50 years ago that management is management. This was largely because I did such a poor job running a university. I did a terrible job. I was the worst manager you could imagine. I learned that one has to know what one is doing. I learned that good intentions are not good enough. And I learned that being bright is not good enough. One has to know how to manage. So for 40 or 50 years, I have been spending half my time working with nonprofits—with symphony orchestras (which, by the way, are the most interesting organizations I know), hospitals, universities, and churches in the United States. If there is one contribution I can make, it is to help people to manage a little better. At first, the nonprofit people were very much surprised. They said, "We run nonprofit institutions. What do we need management for? That's for business. We don't have a bottom line." And the answer: "Precisely because you don't have a bottom line, you need management all the more."

And so how do you appraise your performance? I'm going home next Tuesday and then immediately to Washington to a conference at which we will introduce what we have been working on in a small group. We call it the Drucker Foundation Self-Assessment Tool for nonprofit organizations [the latest incarnation of which is the book *The Five Most Important Questions You Will Ever Ask About Your Organization*]. Here too, the question is asked, "What are results for us in this organization?" It is a very tough question to answer for the hospital or for the community organization. And yet it is crucial. Good intentions are not good enough. Good intentions only waste time. The most precious commodity, in addition to money, is the goodwill and hard work of volunteers. So we have to learn how to manage them.

There are limitations. The first one is don't try to do too many things. Try to concentrate on one thing. And the second one is do it well. You manage for results; you don't manage for good intentions. The third thing to say is that you have two constituencies. One is the people who benefit from what you are doing. But the other consists of the people who work for you—especially the volunteers. If you do a good job, you may do more for them than you do for your beneficiaries. This is, in part, because they learn so much. And it's partly because it means so much to them. They can see results.

Here is a daughter of mine who is hard working in her job, who is married and has two children of her own, and so I asked, "How can you spend two evenings a week on that school board of yours?" And she said, "You know I have a wonderful job. But at the bank, I am so far away from results. I don't see what I contribute. On that school board, I see it the next week." And that is what one hears again and again.

From a talk delivered during a symposium in Tokyo.

20

The Knowledge Worker
and the Knowledge Society

1994

The knowledge society is an employee society. Traditional society—or society before the rise of the manufacturing enterprise and the blue-collar manufacturing worker—was not a society of independents. Thomas Jefferson's society of independent, small farmers each being the owner of his own family farm, and farming it without any help except that of his wife and his children, was never much more than a fantasy. Most people in history were dependents. But they did not work for an organization. They were working for an owner, as slaves, as serfs, as hired hands on the farm; as journeymen and apprentices in the craftsmen's shops; as shop assistants and salespeople for a merchant; as domestic servants, free or unfree; and so on. They worked for a master. When blue-collar work in manufacturing first arose they still worked for a master.

In Dickens's great 1854 novel of a bitter labor conflict in a cotton mill [*Hard Times*], the workers worked for an owner. They did not work for the factory. Only late in the nineteenth century did the factory rather than the owner become the employer. And only in the twentieth century did the corporation, rather than the factory, then become the employer. Only in this century has the master been replaced by a boss, who himself, 99 times out of 100, is an employee and has a boss.

Knowledge workers will be both employees who have a boss and bosses who have employees.

Organizations were not known to yesterday's social science, and they are, by and large, not yet known to today's social science. The great German sociologist Ferdinand Toennies, in his 1888 book *Gemeinschaft und Gesellschaft* [Community and Society] classified the known forms of human organization as being either community, which is organic, and fate, or society, which is a structure and very largely under social control. He never talked of organization. Nor did any of the other sociologists of the nineteenth or early twentieth century.

But organization is neither community nor society, although it partakes of some characteristics of each. It is not fate. Membership in an organization is always freely chosen. One joins a company or a government agency or the teaching staff of a university. One is not born into it. And one can always leave. It is not society, either, especially as it does not embrace the totality of its members. The director of market research in a company is also a member of half a dozen other organizations. She may belong to a church, to a tennis club, and may well spend, especially if an American, five hours a week as a volunteer for a local nonprofit organization—for example, as a leader of a Girl Scout troop. Organizations, in other words, are not true collectives. They are tools—means to an end.

There have been earlier organizations. The professional military as it arose after the seventeenth century was an organization; it was neither a society nor a community. The modern university, as it emerged after the foundation of the University of Berlin in 1809, was an organization. Faculty members freely joined and could always leave. The same can be said for the civil service as it arose in the eighteenth century, first in France, then on the European continent, and finally in late nineteenth century in Great Britain and *Meiji* Japan (though not until 1933 or World War II in the United States).

But these earlier organizations were still seen as exceptions. The first organization in the modern sense, the first that was seen as being prototypical rather than exceptional, was surely the modern business enterprise as it emerged after 1870, which is the reason why, to this day, most people think of management as being "business management."

With the emergence of the knowledge society, society has become a society of organizations. Most of us work in and for an organization, and we are dependent for our effectiveness and equally for our living on access to an organization, whether as an organization's employee or as a provider of services to an organization—as a lawyer, for instance, or a freight forwarder. More and more of these supporting services to organizations are, themselves, organized as organizations. The first law firm was organized in the United States a little over a century ago; until then, lawyers practiced as individuals. In Europe there were no law firms to speak of until after World War II. Today, the practice of law is increasingly done in larger and larger partnerships. It is also true, especially in the United States, of the practice of medicine. The knowledge society is a society of organizations in which practically every single task is being performed in and through an organization.

Most knowledge workers will spend most if not all of their working life as employees. The meaning of the term is different from what it has been traditionally, and not only in English but in German, Spanish, or Japanese as well.

Individually, knowledge workers are dependent on the job. They receive a wage or salary. They are being hired and can be fired. Legally, each is an employee. But, collectively, they are the only capitalists. Increasingly, through their pension funds and through their other savings (such as through mutual funds in the United States), the employees own the means of production. In traditional economics—and by no means only in Marxist economics—there is a sharp distinction between the wage fund, all of which goes into consumption, and the capital fund. Most social theory of industrial society is based, one way or another, on the relationship between the two, whether in conflict or in necessary and beneficial cooperation and balance. In the knowledge society, the two merge. The pension fund is deferred wages and, as such, a wage fund. It is also increasingly the main source of capital, if not the only source of capital, for the knowledge society.

Equally important, perhaps more important: In the knowledge society, the employees—that is, knowledge workers—again own the tools of production. Marx's great insight was the realization that the factory worker does not and cannot own the tools of production and therefore has to be alienated. There was no way, Marx pointed out, for the worker to own the steam engine and to be able to take the steam engine with him when moving from one job to another. The capitalist had to own the steam engine and had to control it. Increasingly, the true investment in the knowledge society is not in machines and tools. It is in the knowledge of the knowledge worker. Without it, the machines, no matter how advanced and sophisticated, are unproductive.

The market researcher needs a computer. But increasingly, this is the researcher's own personal computer—a cheap tool the market researcher takes along wherever he or she goes. And the true capital equipment of market research is the knowledge of markets, of statistics, and of the application of market research to business strategy, which is lodged between the researcher's ears and is his or her exclusive and inalienable property. The surgeon needs the operating room of the hospital and all of its expensive capital equipment. But the surgeon's true capital investment is the 12 or 15 years of training and the resulting knowledge that the surgeon takes from one hospital to the next. Without that knowledge, the hospital's expensive operating rooms are so much waste and scrap.

This is true whether the knowledge worker commands advanced knowledge, like the surgeon, or simple and fairly elementary knowledge like the junior accountant. In either case, it is the knowledge investment that determines whether the employee is productive—not the tools, machines, and capital the organization furnishes.

The industrial worker needed the capitalist infinitely more than the capitalist needed the industrial worker—the basis for Marx's assertion that there would always be a surplus of industrial workers, an industrial reserve army that would make sure wages could not possibly rise above the subsistence level (probably Marx's most egregious error). In the knowledge society the most probable assumption, and certainly the assumption on which all organizations have to conduct their affairs, is that they need the knowledge worker far more than the knowledge worker needs them. It is the organization's job to market its knowledge jobs so as to obtain knowledge workers in adequate quantity and superior quality. The relationship increasingly is one of interdependence, with the knowledge worker having to learn what the organization needs, but with the organization also having to learn what the knowledge workers needs, requires, and expects.

Because its work is based on knowledge, the knowledge organization is altogether not one of superiors and subordinates. The prototype is the symphony orchestra. The first violin may be the most important instrument in the orchestra. But the first violinist is not the superior of the harp player. He is a colleague. The harp part is the harp player's part, and not delegated to her by either the conductor or the first violinist.

There was endless debate in the Middle Ages about the hierarchy of knowledges, with philosophy claiming to be the queen of knowledges. We long ago gave up that moot argument. There is no higher knowledge and no lower knowledge. When the patient's complaint is an ingrown toenail, the podiatrist's knowledge controls, and not that of the brain surgeon—even though the brain surgeon represents many more years of training and gets a much larger fee. If an executive is posted to a foreign country, the knowledge he or she needs, and in a hurry, is the fairly low skill of acquiring fluency in a foreign language—something every native of that country has mastered by age 2 without any great investment. The knowledge of the knowledge society, precisely because it is knowledge only when applied in action, derives its rank and standing from the situation and not from its knowledge content. This, too, is new. Knowledges were always seen as fixed stars, so to speak, each occupying its own position in the universe of knowledge. In the knowledge society, knowledges are tools and, as such, dependent for their importance and position on the task to be performed.

One final conclusion: Because the knowledge society perforce has to be a society of organizations, its central and distinctive organ is management.

When we first began to talk of management, the term meant business management. But we have learned in this last half century that management is the distinctive organ of all organizations. All of them require management, whether they use the term or not. All managers do the same things, whatever the business of their organization. All of them have to bring people—each of them possessing a different knowledge—together for joint performance. All of them have to make human strengths productive in performance and human weaknesses irrelevant. All of them have to think through what are results in the organization, and all of them have to define objectives. All of them are responsible to think through what I call "the theory of the business"—that is, the assumptions on which the organization bases its performance and actions, and equally, the assumptions on which organizations decide what things not to do.

All of them require an organ that thinks through strategies— that is, the means through which the goals of the organization become performance. All of them have to define the values of the organization: its system of rewards and punishments, and its spirit and its culture. In all of them, managers need both the knowledge of management as work and discipline and the knowledge and understanding of the organization itself—its purposes, its values, its environment and markets, its core competencies.

Management as a practice is very old. The most successful executive in all history was surely that Egyptian who, 4,000 years ago or more, first conceived the pyramid without any precedent, designed and built it, and did so in record time. Unlike any other work of man, that first pyramid still stands. But as a discipline, management is barely 50 years old. It was first dimly perceived around the time of World War I. It did not emerge until World War II, and then primarily in the United States. Since then, it has been the fastest-growing new function, and its study the fastest-growing new discipline. No function in history has emerged as fast as management, and surely none has had such worldwide sweep in such a short period.

Management, in most business schools, is still taught as a bundle of techniques—budgeting or organization development. To be sure, management, like any other work, has its own tools and its own techniques. But just as the essence of medicine is not the urine analysis, the essence of management is not technique or procedure. The essence of management is to make knowledges productive. Management, in other words, is a social function. And, in its practice, management is truly a liberal art.

From the Edwin L. Godkin Lecture at Harvard University.

21

Reinventing Government:
The Next Phase

1994

It is a great pleasure and a great privilege to speak to such a distinguished group and on so important a subject. My title, as you know, is "Reinventing Government: The Next Phase." My topic is: how to build on your achievement. It is a remarkable and substantial achievement. But is it also a fragile one. It is a first step.

What comes now is both to consolidate what has been achieved so far and to break through to a new dimension of achievement. But before I begin, one caveat: You who are listening to me today, you government people, emphasize the word *government* in "reinventing government." My emphasis has to be on the word *reinventing*. Of that, I know a little bit, having worked for half a century with all kinds of organizations—a good many government agencies and state governments, both U.S. and foreign (the United Kingdom, Canada, Japan); with our own military many years back; with businesses and labor unions; with churches and hospitals—on repositioning themselves. It's a term I prefer to what you call "reinventing themselves."

But of government, and especially the entirety of the federal government, I speak as an outsider, and with considerable trepidation. I simply don't know enough firsthand about the federal government. There was a time when I did a good deal with and for the federal government. In fact, both Mr. Truman and Mr. Eisenhower wanted me to join their administrations in a sub-cabinet position. I had to say "no" because I've known for a long time that I don't function in a big organization; I only do damage. Altogether, all my work for the federal government and for any other government—state or local, domestic or foreign—has been as an advisor, as a friend, and on special assignments. And I have never taken any pay from any government. But, above all, my government experience, such as it is, is a long way back. My last substantial government assignments were in the very early Kennedy years. And so I'm quite apprehensive to speak to a group of real experts. And I therefore ask in advance for your indulgence for my ignorance. I am sure that I will say a good many things that will appear to you experts as very naive indeed.

But being an outsider also has certain advantages. The outsider doesn't know the details. And while there is truth in the old saying that "God is in the details," it's also true that details alone are treacherous. You need to see the big picture, as well—and that the outsider often sees more clearly.

You insiders are also totally absorbed in day-to-day work on specific projects. And, as I long ago learned, anything that degenerates into work takes time and effort and total attention. And then, it is very easy to forget tomorrow because today is already overloaded. The outsider, by contrast, is free from such nasty and disconcerting things as having to do work and having to produce results. Unlike the insider, the outsider is not inhibited by knowing all the things that cannot be done.

And I am going to talk today about things that most of you insiders know cannot be done—even though most of you also know that they must be done. When Vice President Gore announced the initiative to "reinvent government" a year and a half ago, the reaction nationwide was a big yawn that, bluntly, was the reaction also in most of the federal government, even within Washington. I would hazard the guess that it was the reaction of a good many of the people who are now converts and who sit in this room. For them, as heads of major government activities, they'd felt as though they had heard all this before. In fact, even when the vice president published last September the first specific report, most people felt, "We have heard all of this before, and nothing has ever happened." One of my friends, who is pretty high up in the federal government and who for years has been trying to do what you now call "reinventing government," commented to me in private, "Alas, this reads almost like the Grace Report of 10 years ago, and will have similar non-results." And yet, you have had tremendous results.

But one thing has not changed, and it is important to realize it. The country as a whole—and as far as my own totally unscientific sample goes, this includes a good many of the people in the lower rungs of government service—still pay little attention to what you are doing. Outside of Washington, for instance, I've hardly seen the slightest reference to it in the media. Why is that? The performance is there, and it is very impressive. But why is it still not seen as an achievement? I think this is a very important question because it gives you a clue as to what the next stage of the work has to be.

If you ask me why you have been successful, the answer is easy. You have been successful because you have focused on performance. To be sure, you are stressing cost reduction, and the proposals that you are now including in the 1995 budget talk a great deal about getting rid of the expenditures that are no longer needed. I can only say that I hope you will have better luck getting these things through the Congress than any of your predecessors had. And, as you know, a good many of them proposed getting rid of exactly the same expenditures and programs, which, if they ever served any purpose, surely no longer do. But your main focus has been on performance—on enabling this office and that agency to serve its customers better; on enabling the Ex-Im Bank [the Export-Import Bank of the United States] to help the small and medium-sized American company to become a successful, competitor on the world markets; on having better training here and better performance evaluation there. And this is what is true achievement. The individual changes probably do not amount to much. There is a long and slow learning curve in such matters. But the enormous achievement—and I don't think it is possible to overrate it—is that you have created receptivity and responsibility throughout the federal establishment, or at least throughout a good part of it.

This is enormous. But why, then, has it not received attention? It's precisely because it is improvement. It is improvement of things that are already being done. And it is improvement of individual, isolated operations. This is how one begins. But it is just good intentions unless it becomes permanent, organized, self-generated habit. If I may use a metaphor, you have scattered seeds. A good many of them are showing their first seedlings. But a lot of seedlings do not make a crop.

Let me be very blunt. I was amused when I read the press release about the performance at the Ex-Im Bank. For the very achievements that it announced were ones that I discussed at least 20 years ago with a then newly appointed director of the Ex-Im Bank, an old friend of mine. And he proudly reported to me that he had done exactly what you now report having done in 1993 and 1994. Both reports were true. He had actually done it. But a few years later it had disappeared again. And it disappeared because he did not succeed—I do not know whether he even tried—to instill in his organization the habit of continuous improvement with clear goals, with clear direction, with organized measurement.

The next stage is to move from isolated achievements, needed though they are, to the habit of continuous improvement throughout the agencies of the federal government. We know how to do this. But it is not what you are doing now. It requires a different organization. It requires, above all, specific goals of improvement—3 or 4 or 5 percent each year—for each agency. It requires measurements. It requires benchmarking.

Benchmarking, of course, is not new. The U.S. Navy, for instance, has benchmarked its gunnery performance for at least a hundred years, and gunnery competitions go back to the British at least a hundred years before that. But benchmarking today does not only mean comparing operations with the best that happens within a given agency. It means comparing what one does with the best that is being done anyplace, and especially with the best of what is being done outside. And by that token, the things you report as major achievements in government agencies would be considered more or less clerical adjustments in a good many outside institutions, and not only in business but in a great many nonprofit organizations as well.

In other words, you have created receptivity and that is by no means a small achievement. You have shown examples of success, and that, too, is a major achievement and a necessary one. But how do you now convert these promises into performance? For without an organized, systematic, continuous, and ongoing process—and without measurements that hold what an individual agency does against the best, the very best that anyone, inside and outside the federal government, does—these are only promises. And the seedlings, no matter how lush and green they look today, are bound to wither and shrivel up.

We need "reinventing government." If we do not make a start on it, then pretty soon we face catastrophe within the next 10 years or so. In the presidential election in 1992, Mr. [Ross] Perot—remember him?—won almost one-fifth of the vote. And he would have gotten much more had he not turned off a great many of us with his demagoguery. A different candidate, out to downsize government, might well have carried the day. And the one-fifth of the American electorate that voted for Mr. Perot made it very clear that they did not greatly care what part of the government would be downsized, as long as the government would be downsized, as long as the deficit would be cut—and without additional taxes. The danger here is very great that government will be exposed to something very similar to what has happened in a lot of big companies. I call it "amputation without diagnosis." In a lot of big companies, there has been wide slashing without any clear idea of what to slash, why to slash, and what to keep. The results have been very unsatisfactory. In big company after big company, you have an announcement in one year that the company would lay off 12,000 people—and a year later comes the second announcement that it will lay off another 12,000 people without any improvement in results.

Unless the federal government really starts to reinvent government, we face downsizing for the sake of downsizing—that is, slashing and cutting for the sake of the numbers rather than to restore government to function, to strength, to performance. What is needed for the next phase—and I don't think we can afford to wait very long—is to ask the basic questions: What is the function of this agency? If we were not doing this today, knowing what we now know, would we go into it? Is the mission of this agency or of any of its programs still vital? And if it is, how should or could it best be carried out?

Do not start out with what should be abandoned. Start out by thinking through what should be strengthened and built. Do not start out by trying to save money. Start out by trying to build performance. I do not know how much time we have. But unless we at least demonstrate that this is the way government is going, we will, I am afraid, inescapably be subjected to amputation without diagnosis.

There are the beginnings of doing the right thing. The Department of Agriculture, quite clearly, is asking basic questions about mission. But it is asking questions, so far, about specific programs. It does not, it seems to me, ask the question: "If you had no Department of Agriculture, would we now start one?" I suspect— and I hope you don't mind my saying something so nasty—that the great majority of the American public today would answer that question with a loud "no." What do we need a Department of Agriculture for when farmers make up no more than 3 percent of the population, and when farm production does not contribute a great deal more to the gross national product of the country? Does it really require a separate department? These are the questions that have to be asked. If they are not taken seriously, we will, in a few years substitute the meat ax for thinking. We will not reinvent government. We will severely damage it.

Let me say again that what you have accomplished is remarkable and important. It is the first step. It is time to start work on the next ones. Your success has shown that it can be done. It also shows, and shows convincingly, that both making continuous improvement a habit and truly "reinventing government," rather than patching it, must be done.

From a speech given to federal officials in Washington as part of the National Performance Review, led by Vice President Al Gore.

22

Manage Yourself and Then Your Company

1996

All management books, including those I have written, focus on managing other people. But you cannot manage other people unless you manage yourself first.

The most crucial and vital resource you have as an executive and as a manager is yourself; your organization is not going to do better than you do yourself. So the first thing to say about a country like yours or companies like those represented in this room today is: development. That is a very general term. Development is, foremost, dependent on how much you get out of the one resource that is truly under your own command and control—namely, yourself.

When I look at all the organizations I have worked with over a long life, there is a difference between the successful ones and the great majority that are, at best, mediocre. The difference is that the people who are running the successful ones manage themselves. They know their strengths—and it is amazing how few people really know what they are good at.

Most of the people I know who have done an outstanding job—and the number is not very large—have systematically organized finding out what they are really good at. You do it, by the way, by using a very old method that has nothing to do with modern management and that goes back thousands of years. Whenever you do something of significance, whenever you are making an important decision, and especially whenever you are making a decision about people (that is your most important decision), you write down what you expect the results will be. Then, nine months later or a year later, you look at it. And then you will see very, very soon what you are good at. You will see very, very soon what you need to learn, where you need to improve. And you can also see very, very soon where you are simply not gifted.

There are no universal geniuses, but a person can be very good. For instance, I have seen people who can just look at a market and understand it. They do not need any tools or research. But they are very often hopeless when it comes to managing people. So find out what you are really good at and then make sure you place yourself where your strengths can produce results. Yes, one has to work at overcoming weaknesses. But even if you work very hard and you manage to become reasonably competent in an area in which you really are not gifted, you are not going to be a top producer. You will be a top producer if you put yourself where your strengths are and if you work on developing your strengths.

The second thing to pay a great deal of attention to is how and where you place other people. Again, place people where their strengths can produce results. When you look at an organization, everybody has access to the same money. Money is totally impersonal; everybody has access to the same materials. What differentiates a successful organization from most others is the way they place their people. It is not only that they keep on developing their people, but they first place them where the strengths of the people can produce results and where their weaknesses are irrelevant.

One cannot stress it enough in a country like yours—which is trying to catch up and does not have too much time—that the people at the top set the example. Your company may be very small, quite unimportant. But within that small company you, the executive, are exceedingly visible. Most management is by example. And whenever you look at truly outstanding organizations there is one person, or maybe two or three people, who set an example. And that also is tremendously convincing. Here is a top executive who performs, and then other people know that they can do it, too. This is especially important in a country like yours, which has to do so many things at the same time because you have to catch up with most of the history of this century.

The most crucial area of all, meanwhile, may well be personal behavior, the area of ethics. I am always asked what I mean by that. The answer is a very, very old one; it goes back to the ancient Greeks. I call it the mirror test. Every morning when you look in the mirror, when you shave or when you put on your lipstick, you ask the question: Is the person you see in the mirror the person you want to see? Do you want to be the kind of person you see? Maybe "ashamed" is too strong. Are you uneasy because you cut corners, because you break your promises, because you bribe, because you do something for immediate short-term benefits? Are you that kind of a person? Do you want to see, in the mirror, what you actually see? That is the mirror test, and it is vital simply because you may be able to fool people outside your organization, but you cannot fool people inside your organization. As you behave, they will too. You will corrupt the whole organization.

The next thing to remember is to spend enough time and effort on the outside of your business. A great danger in an organization, and not only a big one, is that you disappear in it. It absorbs you, so that you spend all your time, energy, and ability on internal problems.

The results of any organization, and especially of a business, are on the outside. This is not only where the customers are but also where the noncustomers are. Even if you are the dominant business in your field, you very rarely have more than one-third of the market, which means that two-thirds of potential customers do not buy from you. You should make sure that you have enough time to look at these noncustomers. Why do they not buy from you? What are their values? What are their expectations?

Change practically always starts with the noncustomers. Today, almost all of the industries that dominated the industrial landscape in the developed countries in the 1950s and 1960s—the automobile industry, the commercial banks, and the big steel companies—are on the defensive, and in every single case the change started on the outside among the noncustomers. The department stores in the United States and Japan are in terrible trouble, whereas 40 years ago they dominated retail distribution. The change there also started with noncustomers. The basic theory of the department store is that the husband is at work, the children are at school, and so the wife can spend a lot of time there and get a feeling that she is doing something for the family, for herself. Suddenly, women—first in the United States and now increasingly all over the developed world—have jobs and they do not have the time. But these educated women were never department store customers in the first place. And so the department stores, which of all our businesses probably have the best statistics on their customers, did not even realize that the next generation did not shop in their stores until they suddenly lost the market.

So the first thing to do is make sure you are close enough to the outside that you do not have to depend on reports. The best example I know: Many years ago a man built one of the world's major businesses, the first business that really took advantage of the great change in medicine when the practice shifted from the individual practitioner to the hospital. (That happened after the Second World War in the developed countries.) And he had a simple rule: Every executive in that company, from the time it was very small to when it became a huge multinational, spent four weeks a year outside the company. Whenever a salesman went on vacation, an executive took his or her place for two weeks, twice a year, and called on customers and sold to customers and introduced new products into the hospital market. As a result, that company understood the rapidly changing market.

Another thing you need to understand is what we now call the "core competencies" of your organization. What are we really good at? What do our customers pay us for? Why do they buy from us? In a competitive, nonmonopolistic market—and that is what the world has become—there is absolutely no reason why a customer should buy from you rather from your competitor. None. He pays you because you give him something that is of value to him. What is it that we get paid for? You may think this is a simple question. It is not.

I have been working with some of the world's biggest manufacturers, producers, and distributors of packaged consumer goods. All of you use their products, even in Slovenia. They have two kinds of customers. One, of course, is the retailer. The other is the housewife. What do they pay for? I have been asking this question for a year now. I do not know how many companies in the world make soap, but there are a great many. And I can't tell the difference between one kind of soap or the other. And why does the buyer have a preference—and a strong one, by the way? What does it do for her? Why is she willing to buy from one manufacturer when on the same shelves in the United States or in Japan or in Germany they are soaps from other companies? She usually does not even look at them. She reaches out for that one soap. Why? What does she see? What does she want? Try to work on this.

Incidentally, the best way to find out is to ask customers not by questionnaire but by sitting down with them and finding out. The most successful retailer I know in the world is not one of the big retail chains. It is somebody in Ireland, a small country about the size of Slovenia. This particular company is next door to Great Britain with its very powerful supermarkets, and all of them are also in Ireland. And yet this little company has maybe 60 percent of the sandwich market. What do they do? Well, the answer is that the boss spends two days each week in one of his stores serving customers, from the meat counter to the checkout counter, and is the one who puts stuff into bags and carries it out to the shoppers' automobiles. He knows what the customers pay for.

But let me go back to the beginning: The place to start managing is not in the plant, and it is not in the office. You start with managing yourself by finding out your own strengths, by placing yourself where your strengths can produce results and making sure that you set the right example (which is basically what ethics is all about), and by placing your people where their strengths can produce results.

From a talk delivered to the International Executive Development Center in Slovenia.

23

On Health Care

———

1996

Most of the talk in the country is a little alarmed because it leads with an "American health-care crisis," and actually every health-care system in every developed country today is in severe crisis. The Japanese are much worse than we are. The Germans are probably worse than we are. The British are in part doing very well, but the hospitals are in turmoil. And when you have a worldwide epidemic, you are not looking for individual, national problems. You have a systems failure.

Let me say that I fell into health care in 1947 when I lived in Vermont and worked at a small college [Bennington], and they put me on the board of the Vermont–New Hampshire Blue Cross. And we had the annual meeting, 60 miles north of where I lived, and it was the kind of a winter with a good April blizzard, and so I stayed home. And that's when they elected me secretary-treasurer. And that is how I got into health care. So I've been around it for almost 50 years now, but always on the fringes.

And let me say that that only thing that could have happened to the health-care system is crisis. You cannot have the kind of growth we have had, in which you totally outgrow your foundations.

My colleague at that small college was an economist. He was president, and I was chairman of the faculty, and during World War II when we both had wartime jobs, we ran the place together. And he told me again and again that in 1929, when he was a young economist, the first job he got after he received his Ph.D. was on a commission on the cost of medical care, which President Hoover started. And to my knowledge, the commission never published its report because it was totally unacceptable to Mr. Hoover, who wanted to introduce a German-style health-care system in this country. He had lived in Europe many years of his life, as you know, and was a great admirer of the German system. But Congress had turned him down, and he wanted to show that paying for health care was an important social issue. But that commission of distinguished medical people and sociologists and economists could not find any cost for medical care. It was less than one-half of 1 percent of gross national product in 1929. Now, since then, that number has increased at least 50-fold—from one-half of 1 percent to 14 percent. And no structure can stand that kind of growth, almost all of which has come after World War II, by the way. Eventually, you reach a point where you can't patch anymore. And we have reached that point everyplace.

And so I think what we are doing in this country frightens me because, first, we are patching. And secondly, we pretend that this is an American problem. It isn't. It is a problem of the success of health care. Our assumptions are no longer valid. We have to redesign the system. And I'm not talking about *how* to pay for it; that's the wrong way to start. The right way to start is to ask *what* we're going to pay for.

Probably half of the demands on the system consist of things that are treated pretty much the way the physicians in Alexander the Great's army treated them. Between you and me, we X-ray the ankle more to satisfy the patient than for any great medical reason. But it takes the same three months to heal. And, all right, you can put a shot of a steroid into it for the pain, but it still takes three months. And the same is true of the baby diarrhea and the croup. Treating these sorts of ailments probably account for at least two-fifths of medical transactions and one-fifth of the health-care money we spend.

At the other end of the scale we have something that didn't exist in medical history: things the physician cannot cure, but where he or she can enable people my age to function, or at least hope to. This idea, where you can't cure something, is basically contrary to the ethos of medicine. That old ski jumper's knee of mine—no, you can't cure it. But you can help me get along with it.

In between, you have the traditional clinical medicine, where the great scientific advances have been made. This accounts for maybe 25 or 30 percent of the demands of the system but for far more of the expenses of the system.

And each of these areas overlap, but they are not the same. I think you have to design a system that accepts this. So, what would the health-care center of tomorrow look like? What could it look like? You may notice that I haven't called it a hospital because "hospital," for most of us, still has the implication of patient beds.

In my community, there is a very good hospital—480 beds—and last October I was a patient there; I managed to get myself a bout of pneumonia. And the hospital administrator came to see me and I thanked him and said, "George, what are you doing this morning?" And he said, "This morning I'm on Cardiac Intensive Care, and on Orthopedic, and on Pediatric." And I said, "Three weeks ago you opened that beautiful MRI Center. Have you ever been there since?" You know how much he invested in it, don't you? But he hadn't been there. And he got the money for an excellent regional cancer center. He has never been there. It's an outpatient center with chemotherapy and X-ray. He is bed focused. Yet, when you look at it, 70 percent of his revenues are in outpatient services. And he has no idea what goes on there. Literally not. He doesn't even know how many ultrasounds he has because that is still left to the individual physicians.

Today's administrators all came up in yesterday's hospital. I just reread Lewis Thomas [dean of the Yale Medical School and president of the Sloan-Kettering Institute, who was known for his graceful essays on a wide variety of subjects]. And the great advances in medicine were bed centered in the 1930s, '40s, and '50s. But since then, the great advances have been outside. And so I see the health-care center of tomorrow centered around a diagnostic and research center—research in a broad sense. Education may be a better term. And, basically, the administrator will be more akin to the conductor of an opera than to anything else. He has the stars. And he has the supporting cast. And he has the orchestra.

In health care, I'm not even sure that most of it can be delivered by MDs. A great deal of it will be delivered by nurse practitioners under the supervision of several MDs. And we are going that way pretty fast—not perhaps in a big metropolitan area like Boston, but when you go to Nashville or Albuquerque, you see the hospital there with a rural health center run by nurse practitioners with an MD coming in every week. The nurse practitioner's main job is to know when she or he—and, by the way, 50 percent of them are men—don't know enough. And that is one unit. Another unit is the bed unit. A third is the convalescent nursing home chronic unit. And there's an enormous outpatient business, centered on the diagnostic and educational activity.

The hospital is the coordinator—the place that allocates resources, that sets and maintains standards, that has the tremendous human resources job. That's not the historical organization or the way most hospital people see themselves yet. And I'm not talking structure; I'm talking about the functions that have to be performed. They are overlapping, but they are separate and distinct.

Another problem that has to be tackled is health-care economics. It's an axiom that no organization can possibly survive if it is both labor intensive and capital intensive. This is Economics 101. At the very beginning, the hospital was totally labor intensive. Today, hospitals have high capital investment. And yet, at the same time, they are still totally labor intensive. It violates the first rule that capital investment substitutes for labor. When one of your hospitals brings in a new ultrasound machine for the prostate, you do not save labor; you bring in 12 people to run it, don't you? New people. And that is an economic monstrosity. I don't think we yet know how to manage it.

Another problem is one that the HMOs are beginning to highlight very clearly. You know, in my part of the world, my physician friends all scream because with managed care they now have to call up and get permission to administer a treatment. And then they don't talk to another MD; they talk to a 22-year-old clerk. And they're absolutely right. That is an abomination, and it's unnecessary.

And let me say I come from a medical family, and this was one of the great complaints of the elders of my medical clan in the early '20s [when Austria had state-mandated health insurance]. At first, those physicians were outraged when there was a non-MD with whom they had to discuss a patient. And we learned very fast that every one of those funds had to have a medical director. At Kaiser [which during World War II launched one of the first voluntary prepaid medical plans in the United States] there was also a lay administrator at first. And it took five years for Kaiser to learn that this didn't work, and now, as you know, there is an elected medical director in each region, who usually serves for five or ten years. And so the physicians deal with a fellow physician, and that we will have to learn.

I don't know how long it will take us to come to grips with fundamental things instead of trying to patch. Yet this is what we are doing, and not only in this country. You may be very critical of Mrs. Clinton's plan [for universal health-care coverage], and she certainly did almost everything to make everyone an enemy. But at least she tried a systemic approach. And what we are now doing is trying again to patch, and it won't work. The Japanese do it, the Germans do it, the British do it—and it won't work. We have to face up to the fact that the health care we have today has become a totally different animal from the health care in which all of us have grown up. And then one doesn't say, "How do we change this or change that?" Then one says, "What are the specs? What are the basic needs the system has to satisfy?" The fact that it is economically out of control is a symptom. It is a symptom of a very serious disorder. Traditional approaches don't work.

From a speech given at Harvard Medical School.

24

The Changing World Economy

1997

I will focus on six main developments that are, by and large, not being paid any attention to today but are almost certainly going to be far more important than any of the things you read in the papers or the business press. They are the six major changes that I think will determine how successful a country is, including the United States; how successful an industry is; how successful a company is; and how successful each of you will be.

I shall start out with a question. Is there one additional skill that you and your organization will need, which practically nobody has yet mentioned, let alone acquired? Yes, there is. It is the skill to manage the foreign exchange exposure of your organization. It is now about 25 years since President Nixon cut the dollar loose from the modified gold standard, in the expectation that this would lead to stable currencies. I do not have to tell you that his expectation has not worked out. On the contrary. In no period in history have we seen greater foreign exchange fluctuation.

And we can confidently expect that to continue. For we are in a period very much like the period in which I started work—that is, in the late 1920s, the onset of the Great Depression. At that time, the English pound sterling no longer could fulfill its traditional role as the key currency. And the dollar was not yet ready to take over. Today, the dollar is no longer able to fulfill its role as the key currency—even though it is and will continue for a long time to be the main trading currency. And no other currency, neither the German mark nor the Japanese yen, is remotely ready or willing to take over the key currency role.

Maybe there will be a working European currency in five to eight years, which will then perhaps become the world's key currency. Frankly, I consider that wishful thinking on the part of the Germans. But if and when that should happen, you may have again relatively stable currencies. Until then, we face a period of increasing currency instability. Add to this that the world is awash in nonmoney. Most of those billions that float around in the world economy are money only in the most narrow, theoretical meaning of the term.

Economically, none of those billions serve an economic function. None of them is the result of an economic transaction, whether production or trade. They are the result of speculation in currencies by and large. They are not real money; they are virtual money. And this money is desperate to earn a little return. But it is also " hot money," and as such it is prone to panic at the drop of a handkerchief—in fact, at the drop of a toothpick. And we have seen in the last few weeks how fast this can happen. And we will see a great many more such currency panics in the future. I would say that you can count on such a panic at least twice a year during the next few years. And that means that you have to learn how to manage the foreign exchange exposure of your organization. Very few people, so far, know how to do this. It is not speculation; it is the opposite.

The second thing to say, and it is pretty closely related to what I have just said, is that the developed world—North America, Western and Northern Europe, and Japan—all face a period of growing and severe underpopulation. We face a period in which a dominant issue in all developed countries is a new social question: the growing cleavage between a steadily shrinking number of young people of working age and a steadily growing number of people past traditional retirement age.

The United States is best off of all developed countries. We still have a birth rate that is adequate to replace the population—around 2.4 live births per woman of reproductive age. But we have this high birth rate only because of the tremendous number of immigrants in our population. Recent immigrants always still have the large birth numbers of the countries they come from. Native-born Americans do not reproduce themselves. Their birth rate is only around 1.5 or so.

And apart from the United States, all the developed countries have birth rates far below that needed to maintain their current population. The lowest birth rates are in Southern Europe—Portugal, Spain, southern France, southern Italy, and Greece. They have birth rates of one live birth per woman of reproductive age. That is, they have birth rates so low that for every two people who die there is only one to replace them. Germany and Japan both have birth rates of 1.5, which is also way too low to reproduce the population. The governmental forecast for Italy is that the country will have less than half the population it has today in 70 years. There are close to 60 million Italians now. By the end of the next century there will be, at most, 22 million. In Japan, government predictions are that the population—now 125 million people—will fall to 55 million by the end of the century.

What is even more important than absolute figures is that the ratio between people of traditional working age (14 to 65) and people of traditional retirement age (that is, older than 65) is going to deteriorate very rapidly. In all developed countries, therefore, the support of a growing number of older people by a shrinking number of younger people is going to be the central issue for the next 25 or 30 years. And the only possible solution is that more and more of the older people will keep on working longer.

The demographics also mean that the basic management challenge in all the developed countries is a radically new one: the productivity of the knowledge worker. The developed countries do not have a qualitative advantage in knowledge work. The knowledge workers in China or India are every bit as good as ours are. The only difference is that the developing countries have so many fewer ones. China, which has worked the hardest on building higher education, has proportionately in colleges and universities not much more than 3 to 5 percent of the figure it would need to have the same proportion we have in the United States. And the same is true of India. We have a quantitative advantage. But it will be decisive only if we work at making the knowledge worker productive.

This is going to be the basic challenge in all developed countries. And so far, we have done practically nothing to make knowledge workers productive. For over 100 years we have been working, and with great success, at making manual workers productive. But when it comes to the knowledge worker there is no sign that he or she has become the least little bit more productive in the last century.

In fact, all of our figures would indicate that most knowledge workers today are less productive than they were in 1929. Whenever we make a study of knowledge workers we find that they spend a very small part of their time on the work they have studied for, the work they want to do, and the work we pay them for. Nurses in the hospital are probably the best-educated and best-prepared knowledge workers in the world today, in every developed country. But whenever we make a study on nurses we find that at least 70 percent, and usually closer to 80 percent, of their time is spent on work that adds nothing to their productivity and their performance. They are being misused as low-level clerks.

When we look outside the developed countries, including our own, the single most important event of the next 10 years will be what happens in China.

There are still 800 million Chinese making their living as farmers. But China barely needs more than half that number to grow all its food. Between 200 and 400 million Chinese peasants are unemployed. And some 200 million of them have already left the farm and are trying to get to the cities, even though the cities, too, do not have any jobs and have no housing. And in the prosperous parts of China—that is, the coastal parts—there are still thousands of big state-owned enterprises that are woefully inefficient and in most cases turn out products that nobody, not even in China, wants to buy. Yet the state enterprises employ something like half of the labor force of the coastal cities, around 100 million.

To keep these enterprises going rather than liquidating them creates enormous inflationary pressures. To close them down, however, would create such unemployment as to make social unrest and perhaps even civil war inevitable. Since the middle of the seventeenth century, China has had a peasant rebellion every 50 years because of the enormous overpopulation on the land. The last one was Mao's. It was the first one that succeeded in overthrowing the regime. The two nineteenth-century ones were both put down by foreign troops—Western and Japanese. Otherwise, both the Taiping Revolution of 150 years ago and the Boxer Rebellion of 1900 would have overthrown the regime. They came close enough. Mao's peasant revolution of 50 years ago was the first one to succeed in doing so.

So far, the Chinese have been successful in walking a very narrow line between social unrest and inflation. But with every day the tension is growing, and the problems become less manageable. The one country to watch, therefore, is China. There is a probability that it will succeed in muddling through. There is a probability of civil war, which would be a repetition of China's old tradition. And there is the most favorable possibility of China again splitting itself into more or less autonomous economic regions. In the 1920s we used to call them "War Lords." Now we are talking of "autonomous economic regions."

Altogether, the growing tensions in mainland Asia will force these countries into pushing exports to the West. But whether China and its neighbors in mainland Asia can, in turn, also become major customers of the West has yet to be seen. One thing is certain, however: The truly decisive event in the world economy in the next 10 or 15 years will not be what happens in the developed world but what happens in China.

Now let me switch to something quite different: Is there a world economy? The answer is both yes and no. Economically, the world is becoming steadily more integrated. But politically the world is more likely to splinter. There will be more Slovakias seceding from the Czechs. When communism collapsed, the areas housing nearly half of the Soviet population turned themselves into independent countries. And it is anybody's guess whether there will be a united Canada in 10 years. Will there still be a Belgium?

The fact is that modern information has made global splintering much easier. There is no longer any real advantage in peacetime to being a very large country. That means that there is going to be increased competition for all of us in the developed countries, and very often from countries we've barely heard of. In that sense, we have a global economy. And it requires that you know about it, pay attention to it, and act in contemplation of a global economy—even if your own market is purely local.

The last thing to say is that you, the executive, will have to take charge of the information you need. Most of us are swamped with data. Yet very few have any information. Most of the data we now get may actually do more harm than good. In many organizations, the computer has made management less competent because all the data it gets are inside data, whether from the accounting system or from the management information system. And this has aggravated the tendency, especially in large companies, for executives to be preoccupied with what happens inside their company.

Within the next 10 years the internal data system is bound to change drastically. One reason is that the accounting system on which most of us in management still rely reports on a legal fiction, the legal enterprise. Even the biggest enterprise rarely occupies more than one-third of the economic chain, from the supplier to the customer. And yet all the information executives now get about the company is internal. Accounting is about to change drastically, more than it has changed since GM and GE first developed cost accounting almost 80 years ago.

But even with all the changes ahead, the accounting information will still be primarily about things that happen inside. But when you look at where the changes have come from in any industry these last 50 years, not one of them since World War II has come from inside that industry. They've all come from the outside, and most of them have come from noncustomers and from people who never before were considered competitors. An example: One of my friends from a major pharmaceutical company simply did not know that the basic changes in health-care delivery are in medical electronics and not in pharmaceuticals. This company's executives had all the data about the pharmaceutical market until it slipped away from them. They simply did not know that such things as genetics, molecular chemistry, or medical electronics existed. They were pharmacologists.

That is true of commercial banking, as well. It's true even of colleges and universities. And very few of us have any information about the outside. And so a basic challenge for the individual executive in the individual business is to start managing information.

When computers first came in, I had a client whose name was IBM. I was the consultant to a brilliant task force looking at the computer age. These were the early 1950s. And I was one of the few people at the time who saw that the computer would make a very real difference and would be more than just a big adding machine. Yet none of us anticipated what really happened. We were quite sure that, in short order, the computer would revolutionize the way business is being run. And so far, it has done nothing of the sort. Most of today's business management is still done the old way, which is largely by the seat of the pants. Then we quantify what the seat of the pants has told us and call it long-range planning.

From now on, increasingly, in every organization, the executive will have to ask: "What information do I need to run the business?" "What information does the business need?" "What information do I need to do my job, from whom, where, and when?" This very shortly will show business executives that the information they need most is outside information.

These are some of the major things that are not in the future but are already here.

From a speech delivered at the Jonathan Club in Los Angeles.

25

Deregulation and
the Japanese Economy

1998

All over the world, senior bureaucrats descend from heaven. The most extreme case is not Japan, where only the top people do that. The most extreme cases are Germany and France. Every real power position in Germany is filled by a former, upper-mid-level government bureaucrat who didn't make it to the top and then becomes either the executive director of a trade association—which is compulsory in Germany and has real power—or, if you are a Social Democrat, the executive director of a trade union, with is equally compulsory and equally powerful. And France goes much further. In France, every power position in business and every university director comes out of the government.

So we are the exception. In all other developed countries, the bureaucracy is the leading group. And therefore, as we look at Japan, it might be a good idea to start out with what we can learn from the rest of the world.

The first thing you can learn, perhaps, is that bureaucracies are far more resistant and far more tenacious than we assume. The leading bureaucratic group in France in the late nineteenth century was a military bureaucracy. It was totally discredited by the Dreyfus scandal in 1896. Totally. And yet it held onto power, though unspeakably, during World War I. And it held on through defeat in World War II. The same was true of the military bureaucracy in Germany. And so, perhaps, we underrate the staying power.

The reason is not that these groups are so powerful, but that there is no alternative. In the United States, we assume that there need not be a leading group. Let me say that this is one of the reasons why I came here. I happen to approve of it. I'm all for it. But that's unique. Nobody else has that. In every other developed country there is a leading group, which enjoys universal acceptance as a leading group. And there usually is no alternative.

I don't see an alternative in Japan [despite internal pressures to deregulate and cut the bureaucracy, so as to raise productivity and invigorate the economy]. And if you look at history, it is very dangerous in countries that have a tradition of a leading class not to have one. One of the main reasons for the collapse of Weimar [the German republic that was established in 1919 and gave way to Hitler's Third Reich in 1933] was that there was no successor to the military elite, and the public accepted neither the businessmen nor the professionals. There was no leadership that was accepted and respected.

And so don't be too sure that getting rid of the bureaucracy is in the interest of Japan or of the world. For the Japanese bureaucracy to lose its power position—I don't see a successor, do you? I can assure you that big business in Japan does not have that support. Yes, it is respectable, which it was not before World War II. But it is not accepted as the leadership. Academia is not accepted as the leadership—and deservedly so, by the way. The military sure isn't. There is no established religion. Who is there? And so I am by no means eager to see the bureaucracy lose its leadership position—though it's doing its very best to kill itself. There's no doubt about it.

And now, in the few minutes I have left, let me also say that deregulation is not in Japan's interest—or in ours. I should add that I consider it practically inevitable that deregulation will come, and very soon, but I'm not happy about the prospect. I'll give you a piece of history to help explain why.

When I first went to Japan, it was in the '60s, and I was working very intensively with the Japanese government, mostly on the organization of local government. And I was absolutely convinced that in two big areas deregulation would come—and come very fast.

One was agriculture. Japan was then still more than 50 percent rural, incredibly backward, incredibly inefficient, and totally regulated. And I was quite sure that deregulation would have to come—and soon.

The other area was the retail sector, which wasn't even nineteenth century. It was maybe late eighteenth century—mom-and-pop shops with an annual turnover of their goods of 1.7 percent at times. If you know anything about the retail business, anything under 10 percent is a disaster. And I was sure that they couldn't survive. And the bureaucracy said, "We know that too, but if we liquidate them fast there'll be social catastrophe." I said, "What's going to happen if you postpone and postpone and postpone?" And they said, "We don't know, but sometimes something does happen." And I said, "You are crazy."

As perhaps you know, the mandarin in Imperial China was an absolute king in his domain except for one criminal sentence that had to go up to the emperor because it was so cruel: killing a man, a criminal, by cutting off his legs one millimeter at a time. And I said, "You are trying to cure the patient by amputating one millimeter at a time, and that kills the patient." They said, "Something will happen."

And I was wrong, and they were right. They postponed and procrastinated, and today Japan is down to 6 percent farmers, and what they have is reasonably efficient. And the mom-and-pop stores have become franchisees of the big retail chains of

Ito-Yokado and Daiei and so on. Mom and pop are still in there, but the shop is being run by centralized computers, and, believe me, they are way ahead of even Wal-Mart in terms of turnover, in terms of supplies, in terms of controls, in terms even of prices, if you look at the enormous tax burden.

So twice it worked. I don't think it can work now. But I've been wrong before.

The main reason I don't think it can work today is that in the past, these developments went on within the framework of a rapidly expanding economy. But the main reason why I'm skeptical is demographics. The Japanese working population grew very fast in the '60s and early '70s, and now it is beginning to go down. As you all know, Japan was the youngest of the developed countries not so long ago. By the year 2000, it will be the oldest. And it has a birthrate totally inadequate to replace the population.

And this not only means that you don't have an expanding economy. It will also have an increasing burden for retirement finance, and that is incompatible with the low interest rate of Japan, which is the basic reason for the Japanese regulation of its financial market. The Japanese were very clear about it. Don't ever make the mistake of thinking that they're stupid. Don't make the mistake of thinking that they don't know what goes on. I don't know any other country in which very able people spend as much time thinking through why they are doing what they are doing. The Japanese ministries I worked with and the Bank of Japan—these are very able and thoughtful people. And they knew that they had a very expensive and very inefficient financial system, and that the moment they made the slightest opening to any foreigners, the foreigners would take over as they have taken over foreign exchange. But the main overriding consideration of the system was to provide Japanese industry with costless capital, with interest rates of zero. It became a vehicle to provide Japanese business with interest-free money, which it has done beautifully.

Now, with that huge increasing population that needs retirement provisions, the next need may be interest rates that enable middle-aged people to build up their retirement portfolios. And that is incompatible with the existing financial system, which is designed to pay no interest and to have people save so that industry can reap. And that pressure, I think, may force deregulation.

If you look at the Japanese figures, they are rather frightening. Their Social Security system was geared to a growing population of young people. And it has to be changed to a growing population of old people and a shrinking population of young people. And that, I think, is the real pressure. And it is incompatible with the way the system is organized.

But let me also say, don't rule out the possibility that the Japanese will be right again, and by postponing and postponing millimeter by millimeter, it will take care of itself. I think the pressure is too great, but as I said, I've been wrong before.

And if deregulation does happen, don't be too happy. Because to understand Japan, please accept that no Japanese in his right senses begins with economics. That is an American fallacy. And I am one of those people who believes that nothing would do more for American society than to close all law schools and all economics departments for 20 years. And in case you have any doubts, I have a law degree and am considered an economist. No. Japanese begin with society because the society is so fragile.

And deregulation has economic benefits but social dangers. You know, my father was the chairman of a big bank. The government [in Austria] put him there in 1923. It was kitty-corner across from my school, and so after school I went over and did my homework in his office, and we went home together for dinner. And that bank was the first of the big pre–World War II banks to go belly-up because it was the least efficient one. It was famous for its inefficiency. And every time I go through a Japanese bank I see my father's 1923 bank. The only difference is they've moved into the computer age. But basically, these are nineteenth-century banks the way they are run and staffed, with five times as many people per transaction as is needed—or maybe seven times as many as well-managed American banks need. But where would these people go? That is a far more important question to the Ministry of Finance than the question, "Is it an efficient bank?"

And so, let me conclude by saying that perhaps the assumptions we in this country make about Japan are not the right ones. We assume that the bureaucracy and leadership group is the exception. No. It is the rule in all developed countries. And don't accept that deregulation is good for Japan. Financially: Yes. Economically: Yes. Socially: Fast deregulation would be very traumatic.

From a speech given to the Pacific Basin Institute at Pomona College.

26

Managing Oneself

1999

In a few hundred years, when the history of our time will be written from a long-term perspective, I think it is very probable that the most important event these historians will see is not technology. It is not the Internet. It is not e-commerce. It is an unprecedented change in the human condition. For the first time, and I mean that literally, very substantial and rapidly growing numbers of people have choices. For the first time, they will have to manage themselves. And let me say, we are totally unprepared for it.

A good many of you were kind enough to send me questions in advance of this talk, and I am grateful. But not one of these 28 questions deals with managing oneself. They are all focused on "How do I relate to other people?" "How do other people relate to me?" "How do I make myself more appreciated?" Not one of them says, "What do I do with myself? And how do I find out?" And this is not surprising. Throughout history, practically nobody had any choice.

Up until 1900, even in the most highly developed countries, the overwhelming majority followed their father, if they were lucky. There was only downward mobility; there was no upward mobility. If your father was a peasant farmer, you were a peasant farmer. If he was a craftsman, you were a craftsman. And so on. And now suddenly a very large minority of people—and it's growing—have choices.

What is more, they will have more than one career. Let me say, the working lifespan of people is now close to 60 years. In 1900, you got 20 years. Actually, our working lifespan has grown much faster than our overall lifespan. And one of the first things to see is that in a very short time, we will no longer believe that retirement means the end of working life. Retirement may be even earlier than it has been, but working life will continue. It is predictable that within the next 25 years, even in the United States, most people will still keep on working—perhaps not as full-time employees of a company, but as temps or part-timers— until they are in their seventies.

Part of this is out of economic necessity. My grandchildren will not be willing to give 35 percent of their income to support older people who are perfectly capable of working. Very few people will be able, no matter how much they put into their retirement accounts, to live without some additional income.

But knowledge also gives choice.

When I talk to the students in my executive management program—successful people who are 45 years old on average— every one of them says, "I do not expect to end my career where I am working now." And every one of them says, "I have a Rolodex in my bottom drawer with 20 names of people to call once I want to change. And I call them once every two months just to keep in touch with them, in case I want to." This is not because they're unhappy with their employer. Rather, they'll say, "At present this company needs a good organic chemist. But I can see that in a few years, our products, our markets, are changing where they won't really have a need for the likes of me. And I am not willing just to sit there and read memos."

So we will have to learn, first, who we are. We don't know. When I ask these students of mine, "Do you know what you're good at?" almost not one of them knows. "Do you know what you need to learn so that you get the full benefit of your strengths?"

Not one of them has even asked that question. On the contrary, most of them are very proud of their ignorance. You have those human relations people who are exceedingly proud of the fact that they can't read a balance sheet. Yet if you want to be effective today, you have to be able to read one. On the other hand, there are the accountants who are equally proud of the fact that they can't get along with human beings. Well, that's nothing to be proud of. It is something to be ashamed of, because you can learn that. It's not very hard to learn "please" and "thank you," and manners is what makes you get along with people.

And then I say, "Do you know how you do your work?" Well, most people know whether they are morning people or evening people. Most. But very few know whether they're readers or listeners. And yet the world is divided that way. If you want to know why Eisenhower was such a successful general and such an unsuccessful president, it is that he was a superb reader, and he succeeded as president two listeners, Roosevelt and Truman. And he insisted on trying to be a listener. But he didn't hear. He had to read. And on the other hand, Lyndon Johnson, who was a superb listener like any Parliamentarian, could not read at all. His eyes glazed over; he had to hear it. And Eisenhower didn't know it. And very few of my students know it. And none of my clients know it. And yet it makes an enormous difference. All you have to do is tell people, "Look, I'm a listener. Before you give me that darn report, tell me what's in it." Or, "I'm a reader, and before you give a long song and dance, give me a page or two to read." Nobody knows that.

Likewise, very few people know where they belong, what kind of temperament they have, what kind of person they are. Do they belong in a big organization? I have one member of my family, my youngest daughter, who functions in a big organization. The rest of my family, not one of us can function in a big organization. Very few people know this. Do I work with people? Or am I a loner? And what are my values? What am I committed to? What is my contribution?

As I said, this is unprecedented—except for the superachievers. Leonardo da Vinci had whole notebooks in which he asked these questions of himself. And Mozart knew these things and knew them very well. As perhaps you know, he's the only man in the history of music who was equally good at two totally different instruments. He wasn't only a great piano virtuoso; he was an incredible violin virtuoso. And yet he decided that you can only be good at one instrument, because to be good, you have to practice three hours a day. There are not enough hours in a day. And so he gave up the violin. He knew it, and he wrote it down. And we have his notebooks. The superachievers always knew when to say "no." And they always knew what to reach for. And they always knew where to place themselves. That's what made them superachievers. And now all of us will have to learn that.

It's not very difficult. The key is to do what Leonardo did and Mozart did: Write it down and then check it. The key is that every time you do something that is important—and this is from the fourteenth century; I'm not telling you anything new—write down what you expect will happen. And then come back and ask, "What were the results of this decision?"

It's also easy to learn what your strengths are by putting down the results. And let me say that most of us underweight our strengths. We take them for granted. What we are good at comes easy. And so we believe that unless it comes hard, it can't be any good. That's nonsense. We also don't know what we need to improve, what our defects are, what we are not good at, what the good Lord has *not* endowed us with. Yes, in extreme cases we know. I didn't need any feedback to know that I am not a painter. The first time I took a crayon in my hands at age 2, I think I knew it. But those are extreme cases. In between? You don't really know that "this is not for me." And so we are at an unprecedented place, and most educated people in the next 30 years will have to learn to place themselves.

For the first time in the human history, we will have to take responsibility for managing ourselves. And as I said, this is probably a much bigger change than any technology, this change in the human condition. Nobody teaches it—no school, no college—and it will probably be another hundred years before anybody does teach it. In the meantime, the achievers will want to make a contribution, want to lead a fulfilled life, want to feel that there is some purpose to their being on this earth. And they will have to learn something that a few years ago only a very few superachievers knew. They will have to learn to manage themselves, to build on their strengths, to build on their values.

For the first time, the world is full of options. When I listen to my grandchildren and the options they have, it's pretty frightening. It's almost too much. At home, when I was born, there were none. Now, less than a century later, people have to decide: "Which option is for me, and why? What fits me? Where do I belong?"

One important implication for the social sector is that there is no better way to find out where you belong than to be a volunteer at a nonprofit. My friends in business always come to me with enormous development programs for their people. And I take a very dim view of them. That's because the real development that I've seen of people in organizations, especially in big ones, comes from them being volunteers in a nonprofit. There, you have responsibility, you see results, and you very soon find out what your values are.

We have long been talking of the social responsibilities of business. I hope we will soon begin to talk about the nonprofit as the great social opportunity for business. It is the opportunity for business to develop people by having them volunteer with the church or with the Girl Scouts. These are the places where the knowledge worker in an organization can actually discover who he is and can actually learn to manage himself or herself.

From a talk given at a conference in Los Angeles put on by the Peter F. Drucker Foundation for Nonprofit Management (now the Leader to Leader Institute).

27

From Teaching to Learning

1999

As you know, there is an enormous amount of talk about
schools. I started counting, and I ended up with about 40
different approaches all over this country—and not just all over
this country, all over the developed world—aimed at restoring
the school of yesterday. And I'm all for it. Let me say the school
of yesterday had one enormous advantage. Yes, the children did
learn basic skills. But perhaps equally important, they acquired
self-confidence. In the school of today, or a very large number of
the schools of today, children lose self-confidence, and that's the
greatest barrier to learning.

At the same time, we know that the school of tomorrow will
not just be a restored version of yesterday's school. We know that
it will have to be a very different school. And we know why, and
we know how.

The basic reason is not technology. And it is not educational
theory. The basic reason is the change in demographics. When
I was born, there was no country in which more than three out
of four people in the work force did not work with their hands.
They worked with their hands as farmers, as domestic servants,
as store clerks, in small shops, in factories. And today in this
country, only two out of every ten people still work with their
hands, and the percentage is going down. And of the eight out

of ten—the 80 percent who are no longer manual workers—half of them are being paid for putting knowledge to work.

And it isn't only that they need a very different preparation. It is, above all, that they need to learn something that yesterday's school paid no attention to: They need to learn how to learn. Knowledge makes itself obsolete very fast.

This coming Saturday I will teach—I still teach all day—our advanced management program, and about half the people in it are engineers. I asked them when we began this course a few weeks ago, "How often do you have to go back to school?" And they said, "Every other year, at least, to keep up with the changes. And every three or four years, we go back to relearn the basics, or we're obsolete." And these are not high-tech people mostly. They are mostly people in traditional industries—a lot of automotive, a lot of aviation, a lot of machine tools. And yet this knowledge changes so fast. And the same is true of the physician or any other knowledge worker. I work closely with our big local hospital on the training of nurses, and they have to go back to school at least once every year for several weeks, and every three or four years for three months, or they're hopelessly behind. This is something fundamentally new in human history. And it means that the most important thing to learn in school is how to learn—the habit of continuous learning.

Add to this that knowledge is effective only if specialized. I may need a knee replacement in a few weeks—an old skiing injury. And I'm going to somebody who does nothing else but knee replacements. And that's true in all areas.

At the same time, as you go up even a little bit in organizations, you increasingly will have to relate your specialization to the universe of specializations. The orthopedic surgeon who will do my knee told me that he's now taking a course in physical therapy. He is not going to become a physical therapist, but it's changed so much in the last few years, and he has to know enough that he can tell his patients what they need to do. And, again, this requires the ability to continue to learn.

Another thing: Working life has extended so much in the last 50 years that it exceeds the life expectancy of even the most successful businesses. Very few businesses are successful for more than 25 or 30 years. And yet most educated people who go to work in their early twenties will keep on working until they are 70. And so they [had] better be prepared for a second career, whether it's in another organization where they're doing what they have been doing or in a new line of work. They must be prepared to learn again. They must be prepared to position themselves. They must be prepared to want to learn—to see it not as something they need to do, but as something they enjoy doing. They will have to learn how to learn. They will have to have acquired the habit of learning.

We also know the implications of these changes. We know that this means a different focus very early in education. When you look at the school we have, it started in Florence around 1756, 250 years ago, and it was a school that quite rightly for its time focused not only on base skills but also on bringing everybody up to a minimum. And therefore it focused on the weaknesses of the student.

And so it is today. Not long ago, I visited one of my children and her daughter in fourth grade. And I went along to the parent-teacher meeting. And the teacher came up to us and said, "Ah, you're Mary Ellen's mother. She needs more work on division." She didn't say that Mary Ellen, this granddaughter of mine, is an excellent writer, loves to write stories. She didn't say, "She ought to do more stories." She rightly, understandably, focused on what Mary Ellen needs to do to come up to the minimum. But that is counterproductive if we're focused on getting people to learn. We know that nothing so motivates people—nothing—as much as achievement. And, therefore, we will have to focus learning on what children and adults excel in.

I get incredible, fabulous work from my advanced students because they are 45 or 48 years old and they are comers, or their organizations wouldn't send them to us for a year or two or three. And when I say, "What are you good at?" they usually don't know that. Then I say, "I want you to write your first paper on what you are good at." And you have no idea what an explosion I get because they reach for excellence, and now they're reaching for excellence in everything, even the things where they are very poor. They are motivated by achievement. And this is nothing new. Every one of the great educational leaders since [eighteenth-century Swiss pedagogue Johann Heinrich] Pestalozzi knew it.

But we can't do it in the normal schoolroom of yesterday with 30 children, where everybody has to come up to a minimum level and the minimum skills. Instead, we have to focus on "your Mary Ellen needs more work on division. She is not very good at it." The teacher can't say, "She ought to do more writing." She paid no attention to Mary Ellen's writing because it didn't need any attention. Mary Ellen is good in writing. What does she need any attention for? But we know that if you want to create the habit of learning, you have to give children a sense of achievement, and that means building on their strengths. The weaknesses are universal. The strengths are individual—and that you can't address in the traditional classroom.

We also know, by way of implementation, that in order to acquire the habit of learning you have to manage yourself. And, incidentally, this is probably one area where the computer is a real help, because when you look at those 5-year-olds with the computer, they are way ahead in computer literacy—way ahead of me. Well, 85 years ahead of me. When you look at them, they focus on what they're good at, whether they play computer games or do simple learning work. They manage themselves. They go back to what they're not good at. But they focus on what they're good at, and it motivates them. The computer has given them competences, but they can't utilize them in the traditional classroom.

And so we already know the specs of the school of the future. The focus is going to be on learning. And the teacher's job will increasingly be to encourage learning, to help learning, to assist with learning, to mentor learning. That will require a good deal of teaching, but the starting point will be learning and not teaching. And we know quite a bit about it.

First, we know that learning is very individual. There are some children who never crawl—who go straight to walking from sitting up. And others keep on crawling until they are 3. But by 3, they can all walk. Learning is individual, and learning builds on what we are good at. And this we know is going to be one of the specs: How do we enable children to focus on what they're good at, on their strengths?

We also know that the best way to learn, especially for young people, is to teach. I learned that when I was a sophomore in high school, and my closest friend was one year younger. He was a very bright boy, but he had difficulty learning the traditional key subjects of my Austrian school: Latin and Greek and math. He was a very gifted musician, and made a very respectable career in music, ending up as conductor of a major orchestra. But in Latin and Greek and math, the key subjects, he was slow. And so I began, without any conscious effort, to tutor him. I myself had been a very indifferent student—not because things were difficult, but because I was lazy. Yet six weeks after I began to tutor Ernest in Latin (which I wasn't particularly fond of) and Greek (which I loved) and math (which I was good at), I suddenly was at the head of my class. Suddenly I enjoyed all of these subjects. *Joy* is the right word. And I learned them because I had to explain them.

And suddenly it hit me: The best way to learn is to teach. Indeed, one of the reasons why the one-room schoolhouse of a hundred years ago was such a good learning environment is that the teacher with 70 kids from ages 6 to 16 had to use the older children to tutor and mentor the younger ones. And the older children learned. And we know that this is part of the specs for the school of tomorrow: How do we put the more advanced youngsters to work teaching so that they not only learn but also discover learning and the joy of learning?

Finally, we know that we can do these things. And this is where technology comes in. Technology makes it possible for the individual student to work individually, and work at his or her own speed and rhythm and attention span. Rhythm is especially important because if you violate it, you create fatigue. And so modern technology enables especially young children to work how they learn best, so that they can achieve.

Technology can also greatly extend a teacher's span, the time a teacher has to spend with individuals. That's because the custodial job, which takes so much time, even in high school, can be taken over by technology. With technology, a student manages himself or herself very largely. Yes, you have to supervise them, but to a large extent the oldest children do that, if you use them as teachers, just as I supervised many years ago that Latin school friend of mine in doing his algebra.

We know that the new school is not going to be cheap—and it shouldn't be. A good school never has been. It is, after all, the real capital investment of a modern economy. But it'll probably be cheaper than the traditional school. The technology is no longer very expensive, and it's getting cheaper by the day.

But the main, the central, the profound shift is that the school of the future is one in which the focus is on learning. That's always been the end product of the school. But the focus of the traditional school is teaching. We have no "learning colleges"; we have teachers' colleges. We don't really talk of good learners; we talk of good teachers. We need teachers' colleges and we need good teachers, but we will have to develop something that historically we've paid no attention to: good learners. Historically, for the great mass of students, we aimed at minimum skills, very low skills, skills so that they were not disadvantaged.

In a knowledge society, education has to be the way for everyone to find what he or she can excel in—to set a standard and not just meet it. And that means a different school, and not in its class size. The new technology makes larger classes more productive. And there is almost no evidence for the idea that small classes give better results unless the class is very, very small. But once you have 15, it makes no difference anymore. And in order to have enough excitement in the class you probably need larger classes. Small classes are dull; there's not enough variety, diversity, not enough mutual stimulation. I think the present emphasis on small classes is a misunderstanding.

The school of the future will be different from the school of yesterday not just because we will expect most of the students to have one area of achievement, and not just a general universal mediocrity, but because its emphasis will have shifted from teaching to learning.

From a speech delivered at a "School of the Future" conference, sponsored by the accounting firm Arthur Andersen.

PART VII

2000s

In 2002, Peter Drucker was awarded the Presidential Medal of Freedom, the nation's highest civilian honor. At the White House ceremony, he was hailed as "the world's foremost pioneer of management theory." And given his impact in numerous areas of the field—marketing, innovation, leadership, decentralization, employee relations, and so much more—who could argue with that characterization? But, in a sense, such praise was far too narrow. Drucker described himself as a "social ecologist"—someone, in his words, "concerned with man's man-made environment the way the natural ecologist studies the biological environment." With that in mind, it is best to think of Drucker more in the mold of an Alexis de Tocqueville than a Frederick Taylor. Toward the end of his long career, Drucker was asked to name his most significant contributions. Without any false modesty, he answered: "That I early on—almost 60 years ago—realized that management has become the constitutive organ and function of the Society of Organizations; that management is not 'Business Management' . . . but the governing organ of all institutions of Modern Society; that I established the study of management as a discipline in its own right; and that I focused this discipline on People and Power; on Values, Structure and Constitution; and above all on responsibilities—that is, focused the Discipline of Management on Management as a truly liberal art." About six months before he died, at the age of 95, Drucker was more demure in assessing his legacy. "What I would say," he told a reporter, "is I helped a few good people be effective in doing the right things." Then he added, "Look, I'm totally uninteresting. I'm a writer, and writers don't have interesting lives." Which just goes to prove: Even Drucker got it wrong on occasion.

28

On Globalization

2001

Let me start out by saying that maybe six weeks ago I had a visit from an old student. Forty years ago, he was a young Taiwanese. In the meantime, he has built a very successful business in Taiwan, and for the last seven years or so has been in Shanghai, where he is now head of a very large joint-venture firm. And I asked him, "What has happened? What's the most important thing that has happened in China the last three to five years?" And he thought for about five seconds and then said, "That we now consider owning an automobile a necessity and not a luxury." That is what globalization means.

It is not an economic event; it's a psychological phenomenon. It means that all of the developed West's values—its mindset and expectations and aspiration—are seen as the norm. Note that my friend did not say everybody in Shanghai now owns a car. Far from it. He did not say that everybody in Shanghai expects to own a car. They're at the stage where they are shifting from bicycles to motorbikes, which is deadlier. He said that owning a car is considered a necessity, and that is what globalization actually means. It is a fundamental change in expectations and values.

And what are some of the implications? Let me say there are still parts of the world where globalization has not happened. Africa, certainly not yet. But a few years back we were in Paraguay, which is not exactly in the center of things, especially if you get into the interior. And yet it was very clear that in this desperately poor country with little education, the values are clearly those of, well, the developed world. And maybe in the interior of China, way back in rural China, globalization has not yet really penetrated—though I think it might be getting there. But other than that, this is now a universal phenomenon.

The first implication is that competition means something different than it used to.

And this is why I am convinced that protectionism is inevitable, not in a traditional form but in new, nontraditional forms. And yet it will not protect.

Let me give you a simple example. A few months ago, as all of you perhaps remember, the U.S. steel industry complained about the dumping of hot rolled steel, which is used for automobile bodies. And so President Bush ordered steel imports stopped. But the automobile companies in this country, including the Japanese, are not paying the price the steel companies ask. They negotiate to pay the price that they would have had to pay if Bush had not stopped the dumping. Toyota, for one, has said very loud and clear to the steel companies: "If you don't give us the steel at the world market price (which is 40 percent below the American price), we will simply shift more of our body manufacturing to Japan and to Mexico. We'll cut body manufacturing in this country by 80 percent within six months." And they are now negotiating for the next model year. Ford is doing the same. And that is going to be the norm. Globalization does not mean that there is worldwide trade in goods or services. It means that there is worldwide information. And that is the determining factor.

There is also talk that all of our jobs are being exported overseas. This is simply nonsense. It's labor union propaganda—primarily garment workers' propaganda. Actually, foreign investors in this country have created four and a half times as many manufacturing jobs as we have exported.

Yes, the three domestic automobile companies are shrinking. But practically none of the shrinkage of manufacturing jobs has anything to do with product moving overseas. It has to do with the fact that we are in the midst of a major industrial revolution in manufacturing technology, as profound as the shift to mass production in the early 1920s. When I first talked about it in 1969, I called it "flexible mass production." The name for it is now "lean manufacturing."

In mass production, the rule was very simple. The mass production people said to the engineers, "You give us your designs, and we'll figure out how to make them." Now, you design so that it can be made. And let me say that [pioneering quality consultant W. Edwards] Deming—and he was a friend of mine—is totally obsolete. Quality control was on the plant floor. The new quality control is in the design stage. That is a radical change from the mass production approach, in which engineers and manufacturing people basically didn't talk to each other, had infinite contempt for each other. The engineers looked upon the mass production people as "just the toolmakers," and the mass production people looked at the engineers as "those arrogant snobs." Today, you begin with certain manufacturing specs and the quality specs in the design. And that is what underlies the greatest shrinkage of jobs.

Perhaps what is most amazing is that this tremendous change had caused no social disruption in this country. You explain it to me; I don't understand it. We have had no social problem of transition.

So, what are the greatest challenges ahead? I'm an old consultant, and so my answer is colored by my experience. The most difficult problem I have found with my clients, whether they are profit or nonprofit, is to change their mindset. It's not technology; it's not economic conditions. It is to change their mindset.

The most difficult period of my lifetime was immediately after World War II. Practically all the people who ran institutions were absolutely certain that we would have a major recession after the war. And it was incredibly difficult to change that mindset when, during the years of the Depression, the goal was to survive.

And I'm not just talking of business. I joined a major business school [at New York University] in 1950, and our big problem was that our dean, who had kept that school together during the Depression—and it wasn't easy—could not be convinced that our enrollment was going up. He just could not believe it, and it was absolutely clear that we needed a new building, and he refused, saying, "Well, that isn't going to last; it can't." And he was fairly typical. After all, every major war since the mid-seventeenth century had been followed by a major recession.

And so there was no precedent for what happened after World War II. And nobody can explain it to this day. The few who were willing to accept the facts—like the man who built Sears Roebuck, Gen. [Robert E.] Wood—succeeded without even having to try very hard. But most of the senior management people, and not just in business but also in education, failed miserably and were out within 10 years because they could not accept the facts. They could not change their mindset.

During the 1920s, there was increasing protectionism, increasing isolationism, and an increasing push towards self-sufficiency. And then came the Depression. And around 1950, I was working quite a bit with the New York banks, and they could not accept the fact that there was suddenly international banking. And most of these banks disappeared, very largely because they could not accept the fact that there was economic expansion and international business. So this is always a great challenge.

I am also bothered by the fact that so many of my friends in American business—and European business is worse—have become captives of their computer. The computer is fascinating, but let me say it is fascinating for mental age 5. That's probably the age at which people are best on these computers.

All it gives most of you are inside data, accounting data in infinite detail. And we cannot put outside data on the computer because they are not in computer-useable form. To put things on the computer, they have to be quantifiable. But very little information about the outside is in that form, and so the computer people dismiss it as being anecdotal. How do you quantify what this Chinese friend of mine told me when he said that the people in Shanghai and Beijing now consider owning an automobile a necessity? You can't quantify it, but it tells you more about China than all the Chinese statistics. It tells you that you have a totally different country. It's a poor country now, but it's no longer an underdeveloped country. It's a fundamental difference. You can't quantify it, but spend 10 minutes in either city and you'll know the difference. And if you only look at your computer data, you'll never find out.

From a lecture delivered at Claremont Graduate University.

29

Managing the Nonprofit
Organization

2001

The emergence of the social sector, the independent sector, whatever you want to call it, is a very recent phenomenon. And it is very different from the traditional charity. Their aim was to relieve suffering, and it was good for the soul of the giver. Nobody had the slightest illusions that it would make a lasting difference to the recipient.

Then, beginning some 135 years ago, the idea emerged that philanthropy should have results, should make a difference, and should result in a changed human being or changed community. Let me emphasize that the old need is still there. If you look at the Salvation Army soup kitchen, it is there to feed the needy. Yes, the Salvation Army is also very busy trying to rehabilitate homeless people on the street and drug addicts and ex-prisoners. But the soup kitchen is there because people need it; they're hungry. It's there to relieve suffering *tonight*. That's all it does. And that need is not going to go away.

Forty years ago, we suffered from the delusion that we could somehow eliminate the need. The War on Poverty [launched in 1964] promised that within 10 years, poverty would be eliminated. Well, it wasn't quite that easy. And the need will always be there for as long as anybody can foresee. But that is not the center anymore. The center is our institutions that are trying to have results.

That we even speak of three sectors is a very recent phenomenon.

The most brilliant economics writer of the 1950s, John Kenneth Galbraith, wrote a book in 1958 [*The Affluent Society*] in which he recognized only two sectors: government and business. It didn't occur to Galbraith, who is a Harvard professor, that Harvard is neither government nor business. But it's a pretty big organization. That never occurred to him. And I can tell you that because when we met shortly after the book was published—he's a very old friend, from World War II days—I kind of said jokingly: "There are actually three big organizations in the U.S., and the most powerful one is Harvard." He said it never occurred to him. And nobody pointed it out. That's not even 50 years ago.

Now, what we call the nonprofit sector has no clear bottom line. So the first question today in a nonprofit organization is: "How do we define results? What is our purpose?"

Bill Gates, who has all that money, hasn't the foggiest notion of what to do with it, and so to him the purpose of philanthropy is to give away money fast, on a very simple calculation. He'd rather waste it than have Uncle Sam get it. That's perfectly rational. The alternative to his giving it away is for Uncle Sam to take it. And he is a rational human being, and probably feels that his giving it away at random has a better chance of producing results than Uncle Sam has. Uncle Sam's results are not terribly impressive.

Today, you want your nonprofit efforts to have results. I think the first of the modern health-care foundations—don't hold me to it—was the American Heart Association. But it really came into its own after World War II. And it has had fabulous results. The reason is focus. The Heart Association had a bitter internal fight to extend its work to the whole cardiovascular system. Some people said, "You'd better look at arteries and veins, at the whole circulatory system." There was an enormous fight, because it diluted the activities. And the Lung Association looks at the lung. And the Mental Health Association isn't going to look at anything but mental health. They wouldn't dream of touching anything to do with the kidney. Probably most of them don't really quite know where the kidney is, and couldn't care less. That has brought tremendous success. They concentrate—because then you get results.

Sure, there has to be a need; otherwise there's no point. And, okay, the only result you may see is to alleviate immediate suffering. Here is that poor woman with two small children on the street. And the soup kitchen gives her a meal for herself and the two kids, and a place to ride out the night, out of the rain, and that's all. And the next day she's back on the street again, whatever the underlying cause. It may be that she's an addict. Maybe bad luck. Maybe she's mentally ill. But at least tonight that poor woman and her two kids have enough to eat not to go to bed hungry. And that's relieving suffering, not changing lives. And maybe that's all that's needed. But increasingly, we are shifting to where we expect to see long-term results.

Around 1960 is when the American Heart Association really reformulated its goals. It set results in terms of 10, 20, 30, 40 years, and it exceeded every one of them. But these were very concrete, measurable, quantifiable results. And there are critics who say this is not really in line with the spirit of giving. And there has to be a balance. But fundamentally, whether you like it or not, we have changed our emphasis to defining and meeting results.

Take the Boy Scouts and the Girl Scouts, two very large organizations. Now they are very different in one fundamental respect—and it's not that one is for girls and the other is for boys. The Boy Scouts see the main results in terms of the children, the boys. For the Girl Scouts, the volunteer mothers are the main constituency. Very different.

But this has enabled the Girl Scouts not only to weather the demographic changes in this country but also to benefit from them. Twenty-five years ago, both the Boy Scouts and Girl Scouts were lily white, middle class, suburban. And then you had a tremendous influx of immigrants—Hispanics and Asians— and blacks into suburban areas. And the Boy Scouts have not been able to handle this, and they are in severe trouble. The Girl Scouts had five years of infighting, and then basically said, "Girls are girls are girls."

To this day, most chapters of the Boy Scouts are ethnically separate. The Girl Scouts decided that they are only girls. The main result—and this was very deliberate—was that the Girl Scout troops offered, quite deliberately, a means for that Hispanic mother, that Vietnamese mother, the black mother, to become a member of the community. And they saw that as their first result.

The Boy Scouts have been going downhill in numbers, and especially in volunteers. The Girl Scouts now have almost 50 percent more girl members and almost double the number of volunteers because they defined the results. And the result was the integration of the family. Sure, when you look at their mission statement, it doesn't even mention the volunteer mothers. It's all about the girls. But when you look at the actual policy, it is the volunteer organization in the local chapter that is the basic focus. It is the creation of community.

To "do good" is not a result. To "do good" means giving away money. To make a difference is a result, and that is not so easy. It is also very risky, as the Boy Scouts and the Girl Scouts show you. You have to make decisions, and they can't be the wrong decisions or decisions that don't have results.

Now, we need to recognize that different people have different ideas about what the results should be. Let me say there's no quicker way to provoke a civil war within a nonprofit organization than to ask, "What is our mission?" And that is the reason why so many nonprofits are reluctant to ask it. And that is the reason why you must ask it. Nothing is more dangerous than the fear of dissent. No effective decision can be reached unless there is dissent, for the simple reason that an effective decision is a high-risk decision. And unless you have effective dissent, you don't understand what you are deciding, what is really at stake.

Take the Pomona Council of Churches. Anybody connected with it? I am, but only through my wife, so it's a very loose connection. Now, we have 60, maybe 100, churches in this area. And it's not a bad idea for the clergy to get together and discuss common problems. And it's perhaps also a good idea to hash out major disagreements beforehand, before you go public with them, so that you don't make too much of an ass of yourself in public. It's a good idea. And that leads logically to the step where we say, "We're getting along so well, let's have a permanent organization and do something together." Fine. I suspect that's how this particular council came into being. But they had no idea—and still don't—what to do. You know the old saying that if you lay all economists end to end, you would still have no conclusion. Clergymen are no different. Most of the human race is like that. So you have to be willing to say that we have no purpose. There is no law that says that the Pomona Council of Churches has to exist. It was not created by the Good Lord; it's a human invention. And not all of them make sense.

Let me give you an example of what not to do. The most successful nonprofit effort—and I mean that without any qualification—was the infantile paralysis, the polio, campaign. It had no precedent. Franklin Roosevelt, as all of you know, was stricken with polio in 1922 and almost died. He never recovered. And his law partner [Basil O'Connor] started a foundation to fight polio [the National Foundation for Infantile Paralysis, the predecessor organization to the March of Dimes]. He was a lawyer and knew no science. But he invented the modern research technique in which you don't start out with new facts; you start out with a goal. You basically work back from a goal. And all of the successful campaigns of the last 60 or 70 years are based on it. NASA was modeled after the polio campaign, where you start out with the end product and work backward, figuring out "what do we have to know first?" and so on. And this was the 1930s when it started. And decades later, polio vaccines were developed. And that's when the March of Dimes should have dissolved itself. They should have said, "We have accomplished what we were out to do. Thank you good people for all your support. Let's have a huge bash, drink a lot of champagne, and go out of business."

But they saw that they had built a fabulous money-raising machine. Nothing raised as much money as the March of Dimes did. And so they said, "We can't possibly let that go to waste. So let's invent purposes." And that's now 50 years of inventing purposes. Fortunately, they don't raise much money. People are not quite that stupid. But they waste much too much. They haven't accomplished anything, not a thing, except 20 jobs for overpaid people.

Results are not forever. I'll give you one example. In Kansas City, there's a Lutheran agency that has been incredibly successful with the homeless. They rehabilitate about 40 percent. The highest rate anybody else has is about 10 percent. They look at the homeless and do not worry about the ones where they will not succeed. They say, "We look for the ones where we can make a difference."

Those Lutherans bought up totally dilapidated housing, and their volunteers rebuilt those houses into model homes—spanking clean, nice, painted, and beautifully lit. And then they find the homeless jobs. And each of these volunteers is then assigned to look after a family until it's rehabilitated. Another key to success: Once that family has found a job and is rehabilitated, the agency expects them to become volunteers. That's a very important key.

And it has worked for 40 percent of the homeless in Kansas City. And two years ago, the agency realized that it had run out of homeless. It had done too well! And they disbanded that program. And now they are looking for another cause, and they have turned down three or four. The need is there, but they don't see a way to achieve results. And they have said that unless they can find something where they can have results, they won't tackle it. Otherwise you waste. And wasting money is not even so bad; you waste human resources.

From a lecture given at Claremont Graduate University.

30

The Future of the Corporation I

2003

Just the other day I had a telephone call from an old friend in
Europe, who was my student in New York about 45 years ago.
He called up to tell me that he had just been named CEO of one
of the major European multinationals. And then he said, "Peter
I have a question: Does the corporation have a future?" And I
said, "Yes, but it will be different."

We could talk, for instance, about moving from control by
ownership to control by strategy. Or we could talk about moving
from the monolithic corporation, which owns everything that it
does, to a confederation based on alliances and relationships.

Everybody in this room, including myself, takes the corporation for granted. We don't realize what a recent development it
is. How unprecedented it is.

If you want to understand how unprecedented the corporation is, have a look at all the good business novels of the period
just before it—[Charles] Dickens in the English language and
[Honoré de] Balzac in the French. It is no accident that, by contrast, we do not yet have a good corporation novel, not a single
one. It is too new.

What brought the corporation into being? What advantages
does it have? These questions weren't even asked until just around
World War II. That's when a very brilliant Englishman [Ronald
Coase], who went to the University of Chicago and won the

Nobel Prize [in Economics], noted that there are two kinds of costs: "transformation costs," which are the costs of inputs used for production, and "transaction costs," which include information costs and bargaining costs and the costs of keeping trade secrets and so on. And he said transaction costs have reached the point where they are equal to transformation costs. And this brilliant Englishmen pointed out [in his 1937 article "The Nature of the Firm"] that, by putting all transactional costs under one hat, you have enormous savings.

And that is probably the main reason where around 1860, you suddenly had a need for business skills. If you think business skills are very old, you are totally mistaken. Let me just give you a personal example. This is from the early 1920s, when I was in middle school. And my father rightly decided that I would have to earn my living and that I was totally unqualified for it. And so he sent me, after Latin school during the day, to an evening course at a commercial high school that taught business skills.

A few years later, I became an apprentice, a trainee, in the largest European export firm in Hamburg. And we were the first trainees who had finished secondary school. Everybody else had always gone to work at age 11. And the office manager said to us: "Gentlemen, I hope you don't mind if I tell you that you are much too highly educated ever to be a success in business." And he was right. And then he said, "If you want to make a living in business, you need three skills: shorthand, typing, and double-entry bookkeeping."

I don't think even an old-fashioned business manager in an old export firm would say that today. But this was the beginning of that unprecedented social organization—the corporation—and let me say that no institution in human history has risen faster.

But now it is changing. In what way? For one thing, the old assumption was that you would take a job and hold onto it.

Around 1955, I ran a study of the management people at General Electric. It was a large group. And while a very substantial proportion had had their first job elsewhere, something like 89 percent came into GE as their second job and then stayed there for the rest of their working lives.

That may still be true at some traditional companies, the last of which is IBM. But it's not true with Microsoft. A friend of mine, who is very high up in human resources at Microsoft, told me that for 90 percent of the people there, it's their fourth job. He also said that the company figures on turnover of 60 percent. If I had told that to anybody at GE, they would have fainted.

Another big change is that companies have given up the basic assumption, the automatic assumption, that whatever we do, we do it in-house. The basic assumption today is: What we don't do day in and day out, we outsource.

To do things in-house, you have to have core competence in them because you do them all the time and, therefore, can attain excellence in them. The rule, increasingly, is: "We do only what makes us distinct, what makes us unique."

As for outsourcing, the cost savings are largely accounting fiction. The real reason for outsourcing to organizations that do nothing but manage data processing equipment or do a particular kind of research is that this is the best way to make knowledge productive. The corporation of tomorrow will be a place that finds the outside organization that does a specialist's job the best because it does nothing else.

That friend of mine who called from Europe spent years building competences within his company. But he has spent the last 20 years outsourcing them. And he said the newspaper reporters covering the company don't understand it. Total sales have tripled, while employment is a quarter of what it was. They think the company has become more productive. No. It has outsourced. These people doing the work are not employees of the company anymore. About two-thirds of the people who work for them are not their employees.

The fastest-growing industry segment in the United States is made up of professional employee managers—companies that manage the employees of other companies. The largest is called Exult, and it's down in Irvine [California]. It manages for British Petroleum and Unisys and what have you.

These people are employees of Exult. They work full-time for many years for British Petroleum. Whose employees are they? British Petroleum is not equipped to manage them. Exult just provides labor, basically. One of the very big challenges is how do we learn to manage—*manage* may even be the wrong word—to look after the people who work for us full-time, year after year after year, and who are not legally our employees. How do we do that? Nobody yet knows how to do that. Don't ask me; I don't know.

Sixty percent of the people who work for Fuji are not their employees. And they have no personnel policy for them. And it causes no end of trouble.

So what you see very rapidly is that the corporation of tomorrow has contracts here and minority participations there and know-how agreements. It is a network. It is a confederation. And so you have to learn to work with people whose values are different and whose goals are different, and whom you can't control.

The secret of an alliance is that you start by asking your partner: "What are you trying to achieve? What is important to you?" You don't say, "This is what we want from you." Rather, you ask, "What do you want from us?" And this is going to be central to the corporation.

Another change: Since at least 1950, we've worked on the productivity of capital with very great success. We now will have to work on the productivity of the new workforce.

One area to consider is the ratio of women to men. Look, 30 years ago in a meeting like this, there would have been practically no women. Now, it is about 50-50 in here. Will we men accept the fact that the smart thing is to let the women work and we enjoy it? I'm serious. They are incredibly eager to work. In fact, throughout history, men and women have always worked. The idle housewife who sat at home and spun a fine seam is a nineteenth-century fiction. You could not run a farm unless you had both a farmer and his wife. And vice versa. The woman alone couldn't run the farm, either. The best farmers we have in the world happen to be the Moravian in Pennsylvania, and they have a strict rule that if a husband or a wife dies, the survivor has to marry within six months or you lost the farm. By the way, the Salvation Army has pretty much the same rule. There is no such thing as a Salvation Army captain; there is a Salvation Army captain—a male—and there's his wife, who is also a Salvation Army captain. So this is nothing new.

At the same time, men and women have often done different work historically. Go back to our ancestors, when the men hunted and the women picked edible weeds and took care of the children. The first civilization for which we have good commercial records is the Sumerians. And the traders—the people who transported goods—were all men. And the scribes were all men. But the ones who set the prices—the controllers, you might say—were all women. There is no record of a male controller who said, "Six oxen equal 94 pieces of pottery" or what have you. That was all women.

In this country, men milk cows. In Europe, women milk cows. We don't know why. On the other hand, up until about 1700, there were no women weavers. Spinning was for women; weaving was for men. In Japan, until World War II, there were only male potters. So, historically, men and women did different work. And that is still true of nonknowledge work.

But knowledge work is different. The first modern form of knowledge work to come on the scene was nursing. It was 1854, with the Crimean War. And it was all women. Now, though, half of the students in our nursing schools are men. Women physicians came in first in this country, then in England, and then in Austria between 1860 and 1890. Madame Curie's sister [Bronisława Skłodowska] was the first woman doctor graduated in Paris.

So in knowledge work, men and women do the same work. This is new and unprecedented. It is a recent invention. And, by the way, it has its problems. It is still very difficult in Europe. In Japan, it is impossible. We are about the only country where the problems are not major. In this country, we have adapted to this very easily.

From a lecture given at Claremont Graduate University.

31

The Future of the Corporation II

2003

Our topic today is: What are results? And that sounds like a very simple topic, but I've been working on it now for quite some time, and it's becoming worse and worse and more complicated. And so I hope you will forgive me when I don't make sense because there are some areas where I know I don't make sense but I haven't worked my way through.

We have moved into a society of organizations. And what all of them have in common—maybe more or less for the first time—is that they have results only on the outside. If one of you has to go to the hospital, you couldn't care less whether the nurses are satisfied. The result you care about is a cured patient, not a satisfied nurse. And a cured patient is one who leaves under his own steam and doesn't come back. That's a result. And the same is true of all the organizations in our society of organizations.

And yet when you look at what we have been writing about and thinking about in management, including all that I have done, we have looked really only at the inside. It makes no difference whether you take an early work like my book *The Practice of Management* [published in 1954] or [Harvard Business School professor] Michael Porter's books on strategy. They look from the inside out, and they really talk about organizing the inside of an organization.

And so if you want to have an understanding of what management is and what management does, you have to start with results on the outside. In many cases, it's not easy to define results. I've been working with some excellent Midwestern colleges. But what are their results? Is it how many people get into Harvard Law School? That's probably a minus. Or tell me what the bottom line is for a hospital or for the Girl Scouts or for a church. You'd be surprised how difficult it is.

We know that the bottom line for a business is net income. But what about market standing? That is not so easy to define, and it is changing very rapidly.

From the point of view of the shareholder, the only thing of interest is financial results, whether it is dividends or the stock price. From the point of view of the enterprise, the question is: How do we get capital the most cheaply and how do we use it the most effectively? But you'd be surprised, whenever you raise this question how management differs.

Let me give you a recent example. There are two department store chains that are very similar. Both came to me independently and at different times about what they should expect from their salespeople. One of those chains defined the results of the salespeople by the size of the sales ticket—whether the item sold on one ticket was for $6.15 or for $615. The other sees the results of its salespeople as attracting and holding customers.

They judge their salespeople on whether Mrs. Smith comes in and asks for Betty. Does Betty build a customer base? And let me say that when you look at it from the point of view of ultimate income to the store, the two are indistinguishable. You can't say one is a better way. But they are totally different. They lead to hiring different salespeople, to training different salespeople, and to paying them differently. And the saleswoman who does well in chain A is unlikely to do well in chain B, and vice versa. So results are not that obvious.

One of the great weaknesses we have in the business schools today is that we believe results are obvious. Another is that, so far, we have looked at management from the inside out. We have not yet begun to look from the outside in, and I have a hunch that this is going to be the next 30 to 40 years of our work.

All of our early organizations had one major goal, which was to prevent change or at least to delay it. But the business organization exists to create change and to exploit change. All early organizations also aimed at monopoly. But the modern organization—and I'm not talking only of business—exists in a competitive world. And so you have to ask: What does this mean in terms of results?

It used to be that if you had a paper company and you had a paper laboratory, all the work of the lab went toward the production of paper, and everything the paper industry needed came out of that lab. That was the theory on which the great labs of the nineteenth century were founded. They were focused on one industry, and it was the common assumption that to a given industry pertains a certain technology and to a given technology pertains a certain industry.

Most of us in this room still believe this. But if you look at where the competition comes from now, that's not the way it is.

Today, if I run a company and I need a six-month loan, do I go to the bank? Probably not. I go to Goldman Sachs and sell commercial paper. And yet commercial paper was not invented by the commercial bank. It was invented 200 years ago. And in this country nobody paid attention to it until some smart cookie, around 1948 or 1949, either in Morgan Stanley or Goldman Sachs, read the small print. And they started commercial paper. Or if you look at the technology that is rapidly changing the last of the great materials industries of the nineteenth century— aluminum—it not coming out of the aluminum industry. It is coming out of plastics. Technologies are no longer tied to one specific industry. They crisscross.

And so you are in a world in which your competition is not just from those who make the same goods or produce the same services. You don't know where the competition will come from. And you have to decide to define your results in terms of constant change and innovation.

This is just as true for the community organizations as it is for business—which are in fact changing a good deal faster than business enterprise. How many of you are familiar with Rick Warren's church at Saddleback in Orange County [California]? Rick, who is now in his fifties, has created a megachurch out of nothing by not doing anything the way traditional churches do. Instead, he thinks about the church as a change agent, a change leader, and a competitor.

And you have to define what competition means. It is not what the textbooks tell you. You have to produce results in the short term. But you also have to produce results in the long term. And the long term is not simply the adding up of short terms.

The question that must constantly be asked is: "If we are doing something because we see the short-term opportunity, will it make it more difficult for us to obtain our long-term results? Or will it help? And vice versa."

There's an old medical proverb that says it doesn't help much if a sick, old woman is going into surgery tomorrow to save her life and she dies during the night. But it also doesn't help if she survives the night and dies during surgery. So you have to have short-term results and long-term results, and the two have to be compatible and yet they're different.

And so this is the challenging task ahead of us. What are results? How do you define them? How do you balance them?

I should note that I proposed the first "balanced scorecard" in my book *The Practice of Management*. In fact, the balanced scorecard that is now being sold out of the Harvard Business School is almost identical to the one I proposed, even though these people at Harvard have never heard of mine.

The importance of a balanced scorecard is not the individual items. The importance is that it forces you in management to look at the institution from different angles.

Now the fashion is to look at quarterly earnings only. But go back to the 1950s, when General Electric brought in Ralph Cordiner as CEO. He reorganized GE, and tried to think through how to measure its results. And Cordiner basically operated on the assumption that shareholders didn't matter. This was the realistic assumption since the famous book *The Modern Corporation and Private Property* [published in 1932] by Gardiner Means, which pointed out that shareholding had become totally dispersed, and no shareholder really gave a hoot about the company. If he didn't like it, he sold his 100 shares.

This was the prevailing belief—and reality—up until very recently, up until the rise of the pension funds over the last 10 years or so. Now, if you're a pension fund like CalPERS [the California Public Employees' Retirement System], your holdings are so enormous that you can't sell. You're stuck. Then you have to take an interest. Then you have to act like an owner.

And having these big institutional investors owning such a very large share of big American companies is not a good thing because the pressure is always short term. I've seen more mistakes being made so that the stock will be up five points or what have you. And I think that this is a very real danger.

From a lecture given at Claremont Graduate University.

32

The Future of the Corporation III

2003

As all of you probably know, it is very old wisdom that whoever has the information has the power. With the Internet, the customer has all the information. In fact, if you were to write an economic or social history of the last 200 years, one very cogent thread would be the shift of information from the very few at the top, where the makers had all the information about a product or service. Within the lifetime of a good many of us in this room, the information shifted to the distributors. And now it is shifting to the customer.

But is the Internet just another distribution channel? Or is the Internet an altogether different market? Now, I can only hope that this is the right question. But I don't think I can get an answer. And if anybody comes to me, as a few old clients have done, to say, "Help us decide this for our business," I don't even know where to begin.

You know, those of us in this room take marketing for granted. But until fairly recently, marketing was not a term anybody used. When you look at the history, beginning with the Industrial Revolution in 1765 or so, the steam engine was applied to factory production of existing products like textiles. The demand could not be satisfied simply because there was not enough productive capacity. There was no marketing, and there was no selling. There was only supplying.

And that went on until about 1829, and then you had what I call the service revolution. It began with the railroads. And for 40 or 50 years, the new possibilities were largely in services. The technical university, the commercial bank, the telegraph, the postal service, and the modern corporation all arose not by using new technology but by using a new mentality. This period is usually neglected by economic historians, who focus on technologies and products.

And then came the new industries, with new products that had never been even imagined before—one after the other. This began around 1840 or so and continued until World War II and, again, no marketing was needed. In fact, not much selling was needed. The problem the telephone company had until 1960, say, was to put in enough lines. The demand was there.

And it was only in the next stage when things began to be more complicated. *Confused* is a better word. Until then you had one kind of demand, one kind of technology, one kind of product. Then things began to crisscross. The first one perhaps was the American automobile of the 1920s and '30s. The Cadillac had the same components as a Chevrolet. But the Cadillac wasn't for transportation; it was for status.

That's when selling began, but that's also when marketing began. In fact, you may say that the American Cadillac is the first product that was marketed. And what was marketed was not an automobile but status. The Rolls-Royce was built to last forever. And the early Rolls-Royce stressed that it was the cheapest car on the market over its lifetime. No such claim was ever made for the Caddy. The Caddy sold status. And this was the beginning of marketing as being more than selling.

And this was 60 to 70 years ago at most. And now we are beginning to enter a new stage. We are entering it because the Internet shifts information to the customer.

One of the great advances in the theory and practice of marketing over the last 30 or 40 years has been that we have learned to define what a market is. And those of you who have worked in that field know that it's not an easy thing to do. But it's a very critical thing to answer, "What is our market?" It is a make-or-break answer. Suddenly, with the Internet, it is no longer adequate. With the Internet, *everything* has become a local market. Basically, there is no distance on the Internet. And so everything is a local market.

Now let us go back to what the purpose of marketing is. And there are two answers to it. These were arrived at about 50 years ago by two people, quite independent of each other. One was Ted Levitt at the Harvard Business School, and I was the other one. To me, marketing was looking at the institution from the customer's end. But marketing is also a bag of techniques. And you need both.

The original definition of marketing was "we make things, and the customer buys what we make." But that's selling. That's not marketing. And this is still the way most businesses look at themselves. Marketing starts with: "What does the customer want?" And this want is what is satisfied. All businesses preach this. But very few practice it.

And now we have new questions, which are marketing questions. The first, for this institution of ours, is: "Is the Internet just a distribution channel? Or is it its own market?" GM, for one, has come to the conclusion that the Internet is just a distribution channel. Even if orders come in over the Internet, a dealer in the neighborhood then delivers the car. Now, considering that automobiles are not particularly easy to ship around, this is an intelligent answer. On the other hand, you have things that are very movable, like books. And so for Amazon, the answer is that the Internet is a market. And increasingly, organizations will have to ask that question: Is the Internet a distribution channel, or is it a separate business? Will it force us to change our theory of the business altogether?

Within the next 10 years, you will again see a major change in what we mean by marketing. It will continue to mean techniques to support selling. And it will also mean the business as seen from the customer. But what the market is—what the customer wants now—is increasingly going to be defined in terms of information: what is it that the customer sees, hears, and perceives in that information market of the Internet.

And so we will have to learn to redefine the business—even local ones like restaurants and hospitals—in terms of a market that knows no distances and cannot be defined in terms of geography. This is, I know, very unsatisfactory. At least I am very unsatisfied with it. But I think it augurs a fundamental change ahead of us, not just in terms of marketing but in terms of defining institutions and defining businesses.

From a lecture given at Claremont Graduate University.

33

The Future of the Corporation IV

2003

We are at the beginning—perhaps one-third of the way through—a transition from a Western-dominated international economy to a world economy that is multicentered.

The present economic dominance of the United States is a transitory phenomenon, and it is already passing very fast. I'm not talking military, and I'm also not talking politics. In fact, the more I think about it, the more I become convinced that one of the major challenges ahead is the fact that politics, military might, and economics no longer move in complete parallel but diverge. And I think this is one of the major challenges that nobody truly understands and for which we have no theory or practice.

If you look at the world economy you would say immediately that it's characterized by globalization, and you would be both right and wrong. You would be right in one respect and wrong in others.

Globalization so far is happening only with respect to information. Things there have indeed changed, and those high school girls in Tokyo with their cell phones can and do reach every satellite in the world. The only handicap is that they only speak Japanese. And most of the satellites don't. But theoretically, they can reach anybody in the world. And this is an important change because, historically, all autocratic regimes have based themselves on control of information, and that no longer works. And the political implications of this I don't know. They are very far-reaching.

In a way, information has always been mobile. There was no way the czar's secret police could really keep information out of Russia. Yes, they sent some people to Siberia; they confiscated things. But I'm just now reading a Dostoevsky book in which one of the major themes is that information comes in from the West and cannot be stopped.

So, in that sense, the globalization of information is nothing so very new. But what is new is the sense that information no longer knows any distance. I read a few days ago a very interesting article about a survey made of young Germans who are getting into the Internet. And they have absolutely no idea of distance; to them, anybody on the Internet is next door. And that is true of our young people, too. And so information has enormous political and psychological implications, far more than economic ones. But with information, yes—there you can talk of globalization.

When you talk about money, things aren't quite that simple. The prevailing economic theory presumes that a country has control of monetary policy and therefore its economy. By itself, this doesn't work anymore. Two hundred years ago, economists defined resources as land, labor, and capital. All of them were scarce. Today, there is far too much money in the world.

Let me say that money is no more multinational than it has been for 700 years, since the beginning of the modern economy in the thirteenth century. It was around 1235 when the letter of credit was invented, making money mobile. Ever since then, governments have been trying to control money. But now, it can only work if there is a multinational alliance.

When you look, you see our Federal Reserve and president trying very hard—and not without some effect—to use monetary policy to control the American economy in concert with the monetary authorities of all other developed countries. At present, the United States is a team leader, but it is part of a team.

Meanwhile, it is the economics of goods and service where the changes have been greatest.

India and China are very rapidly becoming counterforces to American economic dominance. These are two very different countries. They are both emerging into the world economy as great economic powers but quite differently. China is manufacturing center. India is a knowledge center.

I don't know how many of you realize this, but India is the second-largest English-speaking country in the world. There are 150 million people there for whom English is not a second language but the main language. They're bilingual, and in many cases, while they speak the local language to the servants and their employees, they speak English to their spouse. This is because the wife comes from one part of India and speaks Hindi and her husband speaks Gujarati, and they speak English to one another. And so English is not a foreign language in India for 150 million people. India also has probably the world's best technical universities and wonderful medical schools. And so India, which was 99 percent rural and is now only 50 percent rural, is rapidly becoming the knowledge center.

We are also moving into a world economy where constituent units are not nation states but economic blocs: NAFTA in North America, Mercosur in South America, the European Union.

So far, very few businesses in Europe have become truly European; they're still German or French or Italian. This is because the European Union is still having severe digestive problems, with 15 new countries joining. But, in five or six years, when it gets over its acute case of bellyaches, you will see the emergence of real European businesses based more on alliances than on ownership. And they will become very real competitors.

Indeed, it is reasonably clear that the economic bloc is rapidly coming in as a new superstructure and as the main agent in the world economy. And we don't understand it yet, and we surely have no economic theory of it. All that we know is that the blocs are free trade internally but highly protectionist externally. We are arriving at a new mercantilist era, with each bloc pushing exports and trying to curtail imports. And we know this policy can't work. But each bloc is trying it and doing it, especially in the areas in which great social transformations are occurring.

And the reason for this is that the fewer farmers there are, the more protection they get in every country. It's almost a perfect negative correlation between the number of farmers and the amount of subsidy. The greatest display of this is in France, where for every drop of 1 percent in the farm population, farm subsidies go up. In this country it is 4 percent. In Germany it's about the same. In Japan, things are not quite that clear; nobody beats the Japanese at playing with numbers—not even Enron. The Japanese subsidize the farm sector by building roads, which nobody uses, and the government money that goes into construction somehow filters down.

If you look at what has been the single most important economic phenomenon of the last 50 years it is the fact that agriculture production all over the world has grown roughly threefold while agricultural employment has gone down 97 percent.

We are also witnessing a worldwide change in manufacturing, which is very similar to the farm work revolution from 1950 on. In the Eisenhower years, 35 percent of the American population consisted of blue-collar factory worker. Today, that blue-collar population is down to around 13 percent. And yet manufacturing production is now almost three times what it was in the Eisenhower years. Mr. Bush, as you know, has announced a manufacturing policy. Really, this is a policy is for manufacturing workers. Manufacturing production doesn't need any protection; it's doing incredibly well. But like farming, it's doing so with fewer and fewer workers.

This trend is also at the core of our race problem because factory jobs in mass production industry were the one area in which uneducated and untrained blacks had tremendous upward mobility. They got very high-paid unionized jobs in Detroit or Bridgeport, and these are the jobs that are now going very fast. They're being replaced by jobs for educated people with high skills.

The agriculture transformation caused no social problems in this country because the people who were displaced from the farm moved into factory jobs that required few skills and paid twice as much. There are plenty of jobs available in the knowledge economy, but they require great skills, and they pay less well than unionized manufacturing jobs. In Detroit today, an automobile worker with 20 years of seniority costs about $40 an hour, if you factor in overtime pay and benefits or health insurance. That's not what the knowledge economy can pay.

So the displaced factory worker today, even if he has the skills, would face a sharp drop in income and job security. And the trouble is, he or she doesn't have the skills. And this is at the core of our American race problem because blacks are disproportionately represented in this group. The fact that one-half of our black population has become middle class and has moved out of the inner city has only made the challenge to the other half more acute.

Everybody talks about exporting jobs. You've heard of that, haven't you? Well, nobody talks about the jobs that Toyota or Nissan or Siemens have created in this country. They are not the same jobs. And they are not in the same place. But actually, we have had a surplus of jobs imported to America. This means that, economically, we have no jobs problem. But we have a social problem because the displaced people don't have the skills for the new jobs, and they're also not in the same location. The newcomers didn't go into Detroit. And so exporting jobs is the wrong thing to talk about. The problem is that the new jobs are not where the old ones were, and they require new skills and new attitudes.

You see that most seriously not among inner-city blacks in America but among young people in Germany. There, they have a wonderful trainee program, and yet the workers are not capable of taking advantage of the new opportunities. It's not because they don't have the skills but because they don't have the expectations, the attitudes. They don't even recognize these knowledge jobs. And so this liquidation of the nineteenth- or twentieth-century factory labor force worldwide is a central challenge. It has nothing to do with the prosperity of the manufacturing sector. Manufacturing in terms of production and in terms of profits is doing exceedingly well worldwide. Manufacturing workers are doing exceedingly poorly worldwide.

The other bit of nonsense people talk about is the trade balance. It is an illusion. You must realize that one-third of our imports are by American companies of goods that they themselves manufacture abroad. They are American-manufactured goods, though they're actually made in China or Malaysia. In terms of the company's total production, these goods are no different from anything it manufactures in this country. You can't look at them and tell that they were made in Malaysia. From that point of view, this is domestic manufacturing. These goods are different only in terms of our balance of trade.

And so let me say, coming back to the world economy, we probably need to rethink the whole concept of economics, which is based on the work of [Stockholm University's Gustav] Cassel, who in the early 1900s foreshadowed [John Maynard] Keynes and stipulated that modern government is the unit of a modern economy. This was a revolutionary statement at the time, and it became the accepted orthodoxy during the Depression. Now, we have to rethink economic theory and fit it into a model in which the economy is transnational and in which the players are blocs as well as national states. These are relationships we don't yet understand and are still working out.

We also need an economic policy that accepts the fact that 90 percent of the workers in a developed economy are not manual workers. They're not working to produce goods but are service workers and knowledge workers.

And, finally, we need to think through our national policy to tilt to new realities in which capital is totally mobile and available anyplace at the same price. Today, the only differentiator is the productivity of the human resource. Knowledge workers are not interchangeable. No physical therapist is ever going to go into clinical lab work, and nobody from the clinical lab is qualified to become a nurse, and no nurse is qualified to become a mathematician. We have a labor force the likes of which we have not seen since the Industrial Revolution created a homogenous labor force. We have a labor force of countless subunits, which are not homogenous and are not interchangeable because each is a specialty and requires long years of formal training. And we will have to develop quite new and totally different thinking. And you can probably begin by saying you can't manage knowledgeable people. You can only help them to be productive.

From a lecture given at Claremont Graduate University.

ABOUT PETER F. DRUCKER

Born in Vienna, Austria, in 1909, Peter F. Drucker was a writer, professor, management consultant, and self-described "social ecologist," who explored the way human beings organize themselves and interact much the way an ecologist would observe and analyze the biological world.

Hailed by *BusinessWeek* as "the man who invented management," Drucker directly influenced a huge number of leaders from a wide range of organizations across all sectors of society. Among the many: the White House, General Electric, IBM, Intel, Procter & Gamble, Girl Scouts of the USA, the Salvation Army, Red Cross, and the United Farm Workers.

Drucker's 39 books, along with his countless scholarly and popular articles, predicted many of the major developments of the late twentieth century, including privatization and decentralization, the rise of Japan to economic world power, the decisive importance of marketing and innovation, and the emergence of the information society with its necessity of lifelong learning. In the late 1950s, Drucker coined the term "knowledge worker," and he spent the rest of his life examining an age in which an unprecedented number of people use their brains more than their backs.

Throughout his work, Drucker called for a healthy balance— between short-term needs and long-term sustainability; between profitability and other obligations; between the specific mission of individual organizations and the common good; between freedom and responsibility.

Drucker's first major work, *The End of Economic Man*, was published in 1939. After reading it, Winston Churchill described Drucker as "one of those writers to whom almost anything can be forgiven because he not only has a mind of his own, but has the gift of starting other minds along a stimulating line of thought."

Driven by an insatiable curiosity about the world around him—and a deep desire to make that world a better place—Drucker continued to write long after most others would have put away their pens. The result was a ceaseless procession of landmarks and classics: *Concept of the Corporation* in 1946, *The Practice of Management* in 1954, *The Effective Executive* in 1967, *Management: Tasks, Responsibilities, Practices* in 1973, *Innovation and Entrepreneurship* in 1985, *Post-Capitalist Society* in 1993, *Management Challenges for the 21st Century* in 1999.

Drucker, who had taught at Sarah Lawrence College, Bennington College, and New York University, spent the last 30-plus years of his career on the faculty at Claremont Graduate University. In 2002, he received the Presidential Medal of Freedom, the nation's highest civilian honor.

He died in November 2005, just shy of his ninety-sixth birthday.

BOOKS BY PETER F. DRUCKER

The End of Economic Man: The Origins of Totalitarianism—1939

The Future of Industrial Man—1942

Concept of the Corporation—1946

The New Society—1950

The Practice of Management—1954

America's Next Twenty Years—1957

Landmarks of Tomorrow: A Report on the New "Post-Modern" World—1957

Managing for Results—1964

The Effective Executive—1967

The Age of Discontinuity—1968

Technology, Management and Society—1970

Men, Ideas and Politics—1971

Management: Tasks, Responsibilities, Practices—1973

The Unseen Revolution: How Pension Fund Socialism Came to America—1976

People and Performance: The Best of Peter Drucker on Management—1977

An Introductory View of Management—1977

Adventures of a Bystander—1978 (autobiography)

Song of the Brush: Japanese Painting from the Sanso Collection—1979

Managing in Turbulent Times—1980

Toward the Next Economics and Other Essays—1981

The Changing World of the Executive—1982

The Last of All Possible Worlds—1982 (novel)

The Temptation to Do Good—1984 (novel)

Innovation and Entrepreneurship—1985

The Frontiers of Management: Where Tomorrow's Decisions Are Being Shaped Today—1986

The New Realities: In Government and Politics, in Economics and Business, in Society and World View—1989

Managing the Nonprofit Organization: Principles and Practices—1990

Managing for the Future: The 1990s and Beyond—1992

The Ecological Vision: Reflections on the American Condition—1993

Post-Capitalist Society—1993

Managing in a Time of Great Change—1995

Drucker on Asia: A Dialogue between Peter Drucker and Isao Nakauchi—1997

Peter Drucker on the Profession of Management—1998

Management Challenges for the 21st Century—1999

The Essential Drucker: The Best of Sixty Years of Peter Drucker's Essential Writings on Management—2001

Managing in the Next Society—2002

A Functioning Society: Selections from Sixty-Five Years of Writing on Community, Society, and Polity—2002

The Daily Drucker: 366 Days of Insight and Motivation for Getting the Right Things Done—2004 (with Joseph A. Maciariello)

The Effective Executive in Action: A Journal for Getting the Right Things Done—2006 (with Joseph A. Maciariello)

INDEX

ABOUT THE EDITOR

Rick Wartzman is the executive director of the Drucker Institute at Claremont Graduate University. The Institute seeks to better society by stimulating effective management and responsible leadership. It does this, in large part, by advancing the ideas and ideals of the late Peter F. Drucker.

Rick is also a columnist for *Bloomberg Businessweek* online.

Rick's book, *Obscene in the Extreme: The Burning and Banning of John Steinbeck's The Grapes of Wrath*, was published in September 2008 by PublicAffairs. It was named by the *Los Angeles Times* as one of its 25 favorite nonfiction books of the year and chosen as a finalist for the Los Angeles Times Book Prize in history and a PEN USA Literary Award.

Rick is the coauthor, with Mark Arax, of the best-seller *The King of California: J.G. Boswell and the Making of a Secret American Empire*, which was selected as one of the 10 best books of 2003 by the *San Francisco Chronicle* and one of the 10 best nonfiction books of the year by the *Los Angeles Times*. It won, among other honors, a California Book Award and the William Saroyan International Prize for Writing.

Before joining the Drucker Institute, Rick spent two decades as a newspaper reporter, editor, and columnist at *The Wall Street Journal* and *Los Angeles Times*.